# Campaign Politics

What's *Fair* ?

What's *Foul* ?

Kathiann M. Kowalski

LERNER PUBLICATIONS COMPANY • MINNEAPOLIS

## DEDICATION
*This book is dedicated to my son, Chris Meissner, with the hope that he will always remain willing to explore issues in the frontline of controversy and exercise independent judgment to make wise, informed decisions.*

Many thanks to the staffs at the Federal Election Commission and the Maine Secretary of State, to editor Mary Winget, and to my husband, Mike Meissner, and our teen children, Chris, Laura, and Bethany.

Copyright © 2000 by Lerner Publications Company

Lerner Publications Company
A division of Lerner Publishing Group
241 First Avenue North
Minneapolis, MN 55401 U.S.A.

Website address: www.lernerbooks.com


Library of Congress Cataloging-in-Publication Data

Kowalski, Kathiann M., 1955–
    Campaign politics : What's fair? What's foul? / by Kathiann M. Kowalski
       p.  cm. — (Pro/Con)
    Includes bibliographical references and index.
    Summary: Examines the election process, both fair and unfair campaign practices, and prospects for reform.
    ISBN 0-8225-2630-1 (lib bdg. : alk. paper)
       1. Electioneering—United States—Juvenile literature. 2. Elections—United States—Juvenile literature. 3. Elections—Corrupt practices—United States—Juvenile literature. 4. Political ethics—United States—Juvenile literature. [1. Politics, Practical. 2. Elections. 3. Elections—Corrupt practices.] I. Title. II. Pro/Con (Minneapolis, Minn.)
JK1978.K68 2000
324.7'0973—dc21                                          99-0344491

Manufactured in the United States of America
1  2  3  4  5  6  –  JR  –  05  04  03  02  01  00

# CONTENTS

# FOREWORD

*If a nation expects to be ignorant and free, . . . it expects what never was and never will be.*

*Thomas Jefferson*

Are you ready to participate in forming the policies of our government? Many issues are very confusing, and it can be difficult to know what to think about them or how to make a decision about them. Sometimes you must gather information about a subject before you can be informed enough to make a decision. Bernard Baruch, a prosperous American financier and an adviser to every president from Woodrow Wilson to Dwight D. Eisenhower, said, "If you can get all the facts, your judgment can be right; if you don't get all the facts, it can't be right."

But gathering information is only one part of the decision-making process. The way you interpret information is influenced by the values you have been taught since infancy—ideas about right and wrong, good and bad. Many of your values are shaped, or at least influenced, by how and where you grow up, by your race, sex, religion, and by how much money your family has. What your parents believe, what they read, and what you read and believe influence your decisions. The values of friends and teachers also affect what you think.

It's always good to listen to the opinions of people around you, but you will often confront contradictory points of view and points of view that are based not on fact, but on myth. John F. Kennedy, the 35th president of the United States, said, "The great enemy of the truth is very often not the lie—deliberate, contrived, and dishonest—but the myth—persistent, persuasive, and unrealistic." Eventually you will have to separate fact from myth and make up your own mind, make your own decisions. Because you are responsible for your decisions, it's

4

important to get as much information as you can. Then your decisions will be the right ones for you.

Making a fair and informed decision can be an exciting process, a chance to examine new ideas and different points of view. You live in a world that changes quickly and sometimes dramatically—a world that offers the opportunity to explore the ever-changing ground between yourself and others. Instead of forming a single, easy, or popular point of view, you might develop a rich and complex vision that offers new alternatives. Explore the many dimensions of an idea. Find kinship among an extensive range of opinions. Only after you've done this should you try to form your own opinions.

After you have formed an opinion about a particular subject, you may believe it is the only right decision. But some people will disagree with you and challenge your beliefs. They are not trying to antagonize you or put you down. They probably believe that they're right as sincerely as you believe you are. Thomas Macaulay, an English historian and author, wrote, "Men are never so likely to settle a question rightly as when they discuss it freely." In a democracy, the free exchange of ideas is not only encouraged, it's vital. Examining and discussing public issues and understanding opposing ideas are desirable and necessary elements of a free nation's ability to govern itself.

The Pro/Con series is designed to explore and examine different points of view on contemporary issues and to help you develop an understanding and appreciation of them. Most importantly, it will help you form your own opinions and make your own honest, informed decision.

Mary Winget
Series Editor

*Senator-elect Robert Torricelli signs campaign posters at the Democratic Party headquarters in Woodbridge, New Jersey, on election night after defeating Republican challenger Dick Zimmer.*

# THE RACE IS ON

As the words "Breaking News" scrolled across the tele-vision screen, a woman in a business suit spoke with the cool, professional voice of a news anchor. She appeared to be reporting on the 1996 campaign for the U.S. Senate. The Democratic candidate, Bob Torricelli, was running for the seat being vacated by retiring U.S. senator and former pro basketball player Bill Bradley. The Republican candidate was Dick Zimmer.

The woman on TV announced, "In another bizarre twist to this year's New Jersey Senate race, the *Bergen Record* [a local paper] reported that Bob Torricelli was involved with an indicted Korean bank embezzler." Newspaper headlines flashed beside her as she continued to "report" on the Democratic candidate.

But the woman wasn't a news reporter. Nor was the broadcast a special news report. It was a political ad written and paid for by Torricelli's Republican opponents. Viewers could tell the difference only if they read a faint disclaimer flashed on the screen at the beginning of the ad.[1]

Meanwhile, Torricelli's campaign aired its own attack ads. "New Jersey voters beware," one TV spot warned.

The male announcer continued, "The negative ads being run by Dick Zimmer and the national Republicans against Bob Torricelli are a LIE. Just remember. Dick Zimmer started his campaign by LYING to you, so why should you believe ANYTHING he says?"[2]

Torricelli's campaign was vicious. He accused Zimmer of sleazy campaign fund-raising and having ties to "mobsters."[3] The campaign sank so low that controversial radio host Howard Stern promised he would endorse the first candidate who called in to the show. Both Zimmer and Torricelli called—almost simultaneously. Stern interviewed both candidates on the air.[4]

When the votes were finally counted in November 1996, the Democratic candidate had won. That election is now history, but questions remain for the future. Are vicious attack ads here to stay?

## DEBATABLE?

An estimated 100 million viewers watch the presidential debates on television, which means those programs reach more potential voters than any single campaign ad or news conference could ever hope to attract. In 1996 representatives of Democratic president Bill Clinton and Republican challenger Bob Dole agreed to two televised debates. They also agreed on a third debate between Clinton's and Dole's running mates, Vice President Al Gore and Republican Jack Kemp. The Commission on Presidential Debates approved the arrangements, and everything seemed set.

Clinton and Dole weren't the only candidates running for president, however. Ballots also listed the names of third-party candidates. Third parties are political groups other than the Democrats and Republicans that try to elect candidates to public office in the hope of advancing specific policy interests. Under Clinton's and Dole's agreement, none of those candidates would participate in the debates.

Among the excluded third-party candidates was Reform Party candidate Ross Perot, who had run for president in 1992. During that campaign, he had been allowed to participate in debates with Democrat Bill Clinton and Republican George Bush. Perot did not

*Republican presidential candidate Bob Dole,* left, *and President Bill Clinton,* right, *face moderator Jim Lehrer,* center, *at their first presidential debate in Hartford, Connecticut, on October 6, 1996.*

win a majority in any state in the 1992 election, but he did get 19 percent of the popular vote—almost one out of every five votes.

Angered at being left out of the 1996 debates, Perot sued in federal court. The Commission on Presidential Debates defended its position, saying it could exclude Perot and other third-party candidates who did not have a realistic chance of winning the election. The court sided with the commission, and the 1996 debates went ahead without Perot.[5]

When the votes were counted in November, Perot had not only failed to win a majority in any state, but he got significantly fewer votes than he had in the 1992 election. Should he again have been allowed to debate with the two major party candidates? Or would his participation and the inclusion of other third-party

*Reform Party candidate Ross Perot speaks at a press conference in Annapolis, Maryland, on June 24, 1992.*

candidates have confused the issues and limited the public's opportunity to judge the two major contenders? Even if Perot had taken part in the 1996 debates, would it have made any difference in the outcome of the election? In general, should the Commission on Presidential Debates have the authority to limit participation in such debates, or should the American people have the opportunity to hear from all the candidates?

### MORE THAN A GAME

Campaign politics may sometimes seem like a game. In a way, political parties act as teams competing against each other. The U.S. Constitution and federal and state laws serve as rules governing what each side is allowed to do. Courts and the Federal Election Commission act as referees.

Teams score when voters cast ballots for the candidate of their choice. Winning means the successful candidate gets to hold public office.

Campaign politics is much more than just a game, however. The prize of public office isn't just a trophy that the successful team gets to bring home. Elected officials at the national, state, and local levels bear serious responsibilities.

Elected officials decide what services the government will provide for its citizens and how it will pay for those services. Public officials must address issues as diverse as education, health, business development, civil rights, transportation, and national defense. Citizens pay money to the government through income taxes, sales taxes, excise taxes (a tax on a specific industry or its product), property taxes, and other required taxes. Sometimes the government charges fees for specific programs, such as water or sewer services. At other times, the government borrows money. Public funding decisions affect which government programs get funded and who bears the cost. If the government spends much money on national defense, for example, less is available for education or health programs. Elected officials make these important decisions, which affect all citizens.

The government also places certain restrictions on what people and businesses can or cannot do. When elected officials adopt and enforce criminal laws, environmental statutes, workplace safety requirements, and other laws, private citizens are required to take or refrain from particular actions to promote the common good. For example, companies cannot just dump wastewater into a nearby river. Instead, they get permits that generally require them to remove most pollutants from the water. The government imposes these requirements to protect the environment for everybody.

Federally elected officials need wise judgment to determine how our country will relate to other countries and what role the United States will play in global issues. When the Serbian government persecuted ethnic Albanians in Kosovo in 1999, for example, President Bill Clinton decided to send American troops there. He also ordered the armed forces to make military strikes on Serbia. Military actions are life and death decisions.

Because these important issues affect all of us every day, the stakes in campaign politics are much higher than those in any amateur or professional sports game.

Knowing how high the stakes are, candidates do all they can to win. Much of the time they use reasonable and lawful means to persuade voters that they are the best men or women for the job, but sometimes candidates and their staffs step beyond the bounds of fair play.

This book explains the election process and examines what's fair and what's foul in campaign politics. It looks at problems in the major political parties, campaign financing, political advertising, and media reporting. It also explores proposed solutions and prospects for reform. By learning about the strengths and weaknesses of campaign politics, you will be better prepared when it is your turn to vote for our government's leaders.

**Voters cast ballots for the candidates of their choice.**

*Vice President Al Gore speaks at the opening of his presidential campaign headquarters in Nashville, Tennessee.*

# RULES
# OF THE GAME

Campaigns are hard work and cost lots of money, so why do thousands of Americans want to run for public office? Many people feel a deep commitment to public service. As elected officials, they hope to make society a better place. Other people want the power and prestige of public office. Money is rarely a leading motivation because most politicians could earn far more in private industry than in government.

Elected offices of the federal government, which makes and enforces laws that affect everyone in the United States, attract the most public attention. Under the Constitution, the president and vice president must be elected every four years. But they are not elected by a direct vote of the people, because the United States uses the electoral college system. Under that system, whoever wins the most votes in each state's general election gets that state's electoral votes. The number of votes each state has depends on how many congressional seats it holds, and that depends on the population of the state.

In the past, the nation had to wait until the electoral college actually met and voted. With that method, it took several weeks after election day to find out who won. With computerized voting returns, however, political analysts can declare the winner much sooner—sometimes while polls are still open in some states.

Congress makes laws that affect the entire nation, but its members are elected from individual states. Voters elect members to the House of Representatives from specific districts within a state. House members have two-year terms. Voters elect senators, who serve for six-year terms, in statewide contests. With 435 seats in the House and about one-third of the 100 Senate seats up for election, more than one thousand candidates run for federal office every two years.

Many public offices also exist at the state level. Each state has its own governor, lieutenant governor, and state legislature. Many states also hold elections for statewide offices such as attorney general, secretary of state, and treasurer.

Local government positions include mayors, city council members, county commissioners, and school board members. Many places hold elections for other jobs too, such as county recorder, sheriff, and even county coroner.

All these races sometimes make campaign politics seem like a free-for-all, but there are rules that must be followed. Specific rules depend on the office being sought and whether it is at the federal, state, or local level.

## WHO CAN RUN

"Wouldn't you be president if you could?" President Franklin D. Roosevelt once asked.[6] The president is the country's political leader, acting as head of state and commander in chief of its armed forces. Even people who disagree with individual presidential policy decisions respect the office.

The vice president stands ready to assume the president's leadership role in case of death or disability. Beyond this, the vice president presides over the Senate and can cast a tie-breaking vote. He or she also functions in whatever role the president decides upon. This can include chairing task forces, leading diplomatic missions, and helping to develop policy.

For all these responsibilities, however, the Constitution imposes surprisingly few formal requirements. Article II, section 1, provides that the president must be a natural born citizen who is at least thirty-five years old and has lived within the United States for at least fourteen years. The Twenty-second Amendment states that no person may be elected president for more than two four-year terms.[7]

Members of Congress likewise have few formal constitutional requirements. A senator must be at least thirty years old, a resident of the state in which he or she is elected, and a citizen of the United States for at least nine years. To serve in the House of Representatives, a person must be at least twenty-five years old, a resident of the state in which he or she is elected, and a United States citizen for at least seven years.[8]

States may impose their own requirements for holding public office. Generally, a person who has been

*Presidential hopefuls must meet the qualifications listed by the Constitution if they wish to run for the presidency.*

convicted of a felony—a serious crime punishable by death or confinement usually for more than one year in prison—cannot vote or hold public office. Basic rules of competency also apply so that people with severe mental disabilities are not eligible for office.

People who qualify for and choose to run for public office must follow state guidelines. Each state has laws that determine when candidates must apply and what they must do to get their names on the ballot. For example, candidates must usually obtain a certain number of signatures from registered voters on a petition supporting the individual's intent to run for office. Candidates who want the support of a political party may need to run in a primary election held several months before the general election. In states such as New Hampshire and Ohio, which hold primary elections, voters go to the polls and ask for a specific party's ballot. Then they vote for the candidates they want to see in the general election in November. Other states, such as Iowa, have caucuses—town meetings where party members gather and cast their nominating votes.

Since the timing of primary elections varies, one drawback in presidential elections is that a candidate may have enough votes to guarantee nomination before all the state primaries are completed. In 1996, for example, Robert Dole was assured the Republican Party's nomination in March, even though Ohio and some other states did not hold primaries until May. Since

*Reform Party supporters gather signatures to get the name of their candidate on the ballot.*

most of Dole's challengers had dropped out of the race by then, voter influence in those states with later primary dates may have been unfairly limited.

Even when people succeed in getting their names on the ballot, their chances for getting elected depend on many factors. Personal qualifications, such as judgment, experience, and strength of character, are important. But party affiliation, successful fund-raising, and public relations campaigns may be just as important— or even more so.

## RULES FOR FAIR PLAY

Elections are central to our democracy, and fairness is fundamental to any valid election. Since its creation in 1974, the Federal Election Commission's (FEC) main responsibility has been to enforce laws that govern federal elections. The commission collects and discloses campaign finance information, enforces limits and prohibitions on various types of campaign donations, and administers public funding of presidential elections.

The six commission members serve six-year terms, with two seats coming up for appointment every two years. The president appoints new members, and the Senate confirms them. No more than three commissioners can belong to the same political party. Since any formal action needs the vote of at least four commissioners, no one political party can dominate.[9] Individual states also have campaign laws designed to ensure fair play in state and local elections. The secretary of state or a separate state agency administers these laws.

The Federal Election Commission and various state

agencies work vigorously to enforce campaign laws. The goal is to keep candidates from being—or appearing to be—beholden to a small group of influential people (special interest groups) rather than to the voters who elect them. Like other government agencies, however, these bodies have limited resources, and special interest groups become very adept at locating and exploiting loopholes in the laws. Nonetheless, the statutes and regulations aim to provide a level playing field for all candidates.

**Democrat Bill Bradley talks to supporters before participating in a presidential debate in 2000.**

*People gathered on the streets, rooftops, and telephone poles to hear President Theodore Roosevelt speak in the early 1900s.*

# CHOOSING SIDES

Throughout American history, campaigns have involved political parties. Most successful candidates at the state and federal levels run with the support of a political party. A political party is an organization whose primary goal is to get its candidates elected to public office.

As central as political parties seem to campaigns, early American leaders dreaded the idea of them. In *The Federalist,* Number 10, James Madison argued that ratifying the Constitution would help keep "factions," or parties, from letting special interest groups control the government:

> Among the numerous advantages promised by a well-constructed Union, none deserves to be more accurately developed than its tendency to break and control the violence of faction. The friend of popular governments never finds himself so much alarmed for their character and fate, as when he contemplates their propensity to this dangerous vice.[10]

In 1789 Thomas Jefferson declared, "If I could not go to heaven but with a party, I would not go there at all."[11] Nevertheless, by the 1790s, the United States had

*Alexander Hamilton, right, and Thomas Jefferson, left, belonged to opposing parties. Hamilton was a Federalist and Jefferson was a Democratic-Republican.*

developed its first political parties. Even Madison and Jefferson became members.

From 1787 to 1816, Alexander Hamilton and other members of the Federalist Party pushed for measures—such as a national bank and a strong military—that would strengthen the new federal government. The Federalists worried that uneducated masses might be misled by charismatic leaders who could then set themselves up as dictators. The Federalists believed wealthy, educated men were best qualified to make wise, unselfish decisions for governing the new country. Not surprisingly, the Federalist Party's core membership was wealthy business and professional men.

In contrast, the Democratic-Republican Party opposed a strong central government. Drawing support mainly from rural voters, including many farmers, the party

supported low government spending and free trade policies. Notable Democratic-Republicans included Thomas
Jefferson, James Madison, and James Monroe.

By the late 1820s, the Democratic-Republicans had
splintered into several groups. One of them evolved
into the Democratic Party and began attracting city
dwellers as well as rural voters. Democrat Andrew
Jackson, who supported states' rights and strongly opposed the idea of a national bank, was elected president in 1828. That campaign was one of the most bitter
in American history. It was also the first campaign in
which all nominations were made by state legislatures

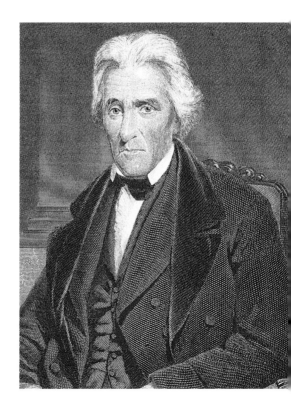

*Andrew Jackson joined
the Democratic-
Republican Party, which
eventually became the
Democratic Party.*

and mass meetings instead of by congressional caucuses. After the election, Jackson rewarded his strongest supporters by giving them jobs in government. This practice, called the spoils system, has been curbed dramatically to avoid abuses, but successful candidates still appoint supporters to various jobs, such as cabinet posts and ambassadorships.

Claiming that "King Andrew" Jackson acted like a dictator, the Whig Party began organizing in the early 1830s. Besides wanting to limit presidential power, Whigs fought for protective tariffs that would favor America's young manufacturing industries. In 1840 the Whigs nominated William Henry Harrison of Ohio for president. John Tyler of Virginia was his vice presidential running mate. Recalling Harrison's battlefield victory over the Shawnee chief Tecumseh in 1811 at the Battle of Tippecanoe (in what is now Indiana), the Whigs coined the first well-known campaign slogan: "Tippecanoe and Tyler Too." Harrison won the election but died after only one month in office.

By 1860 the Whigs' popularity was waning, and the party began to break into groups over the question of slavery. Antislavery sentiment gave birth to the Republican Party in 1854, and many Northern Whigs joined it.

Republican Abraham Lincoln denounced slavery while campaigning against Democrat Stephen Douglas in 1860. In addition, the party platform—a formal statement of policy principles—called for full citizenship rights for immigrants, establishment of a transcontinental railroad, enactment of a homestead policy to settle frontier lands, and protective tariffs that would favor domestic goods over imported products.

*The national Whig Party banner*

## DOMINATING THE POLITICAL SCENE

The Democratic and Republican Parties have remained the dominant political parties in the United States since the Civil War, but their memberships and policies have changed over time. In the late 1800s, for example, the Republican Party fought vigorously for civil rights. Then, when Theodore Roosevelt campaigned for reelection in 1904, he supported much reform legislation. He crusaded for honesty in government and the regulation of large monopolies. Roosevelt promised a Square Deal by which big business would be forced to treat consumers and workers fairly.[12] After World War I (1914–1918), however, the Republican Party championed probusiness policies for a strong economy and an isolationist foreign policy to keep the United States from getting involved in foreign political disputes.

The Democratic Party also changed. During the Great Depression of the 1930s, President Franklin Roosevelt promised a New Deal and pushed for a strong federal government that could take an active role in creating jobs for people. This was a dramatic shift from the party's position fifty years earlier.

In the 1950s, Republican Dwight Eisenhower, a popular World War II hero, ran on a platform called Modern Republicanism. He pushed for liberal social policies but wanted limitations on government spending. During his presidency, Congress passed the first civil rights act since the Reconstruction period after the Civil War.

During the early 1960s, the Democratic Party championed the cause of social change. In 1960 Democrat John Kennedy defeated Republican Richard Nixon and called for many reforms. In 1964, under the leadership of President Lyndon Johnson, a Democrat, the government enacted a federal welfare program, established education programs, and adopted legislation to guarantee civil rights to people of color, women, and other groups.

In the late twentieth century, the Republican Party promoted policies favorable to business as a way to spur economic growth. The party also supported con-

*Franklin D. Roosevelt,* **center, surrounded by his wife, Eleanor, with purse,** *his son, Elliot,* **at his side, and a crowd of campaign supporters in 1932**

*John. F. Kennedy,
left, a Democrat,
and Dwight
Eisenhower, a
Republican, both
pushed for civil
rights during their
presidencies.*

servative social policies, such as tight limits on welfare programs. In contrast, the Democratic Party continued to seek an expansive role for the federal government. It prided itself on promoting liberal policies, including vigorous environmental protection laws and strong enforcement of civil rights laws.

In both parties, however, there are exceptions to these generalizations. Some Democrats oppose expanded government spending and want to protect businesses that provide jobs for their constituents. Likewise, some Republicans favor strong social welfare programs and environmental legislation, even if it hurts businesses.

In order to build a majority and maximize success on election day, both Republicans and Democrats compromise on these and other issues. Indeed, both major parties know that candidates with extreme positions can alienate large blocs of voters. Conservative Republican Barry Goldwater in 1964 and liberal Democratic candidate George McGovern in 1972 were polar opposites in their political views, but neither made a strong showing on election day.

Because both major parties tend to prefer "middle-of-the-road" candidates as the twenty-first century begins, their positions can sound strikingly similar. Both Republicans and Democrats are apt to claim they want to avoid tax increases, fight drug abuse, reduce crime, improve the economy, and support the integrity of the American family. Of course, almost none of the candidates would admit that they want higher taxes, more crime, or higher unemployment, and they certainly wouldn't say they are against the American family.

Differences may lie in how candidates would achieve their goals, however. Democratic candidates might view stricter gun control laws as a way to reduce crime, while Republican candidates might argue for stricter, mandatory prison sentences for specific crimes. Republican candidates might view laws forbidding homosexual marriages as protecting the American family, while Democratic candidates might seek expanded support for single parents. Getting past the rhetoric and into the details of the candidates' positions can help you decide who would better represent your views and opinions.

## THIRD PARTIES AND INDEPENDENTS

While American campaigns are dominated by two major political parties, there are other "teams," known as third parties. Occasionally a candidate will run as an Independent, without any party support.

Specific policy issues can spur the growth of third

parties. During the mid-nineteenth century, the Free-Soiler Party campaigned against slavery. In 1869 the Prohibition Party organized to oppose the sale of alcohol. In the 1870s and 1880s, the Greenback Party called for changes in the money system.

A group of people protesting a secret society called the Masons—composed mainly of wealthy and privileged people—formed the Anti-Masonic Party. In 1831 the party held, for the first time in the history of the United States, a national convention for nominating presidential and vice presidential candidates. Its candidate, William Wirt from Maryland, got seven electoral votes and eight percent of the popular vote in the 1832 presidential election.[13]

The Populist Party, formed in 1891, provides a good illustration of how third parties can affect policy choices. Populists called for an income tax, restrictions on huge corporations, the coining of silver money, legislation to protect farmers, and public ownership of railroad and telephone companies.[14] Even though its candidates never won the presidency, Congress passed the Sherman Antitrust Act in 1903, and the income tax later became law by constitutional amendment in 1916.

Other third parties promote a specific ideology or framework for policy ideas. Libertarian Party candidates seek restrictions on government power and the adoption of conservative social and monetary policies. Socialist and Communist Party candidates stand on the opposite end of the political spectrum, urging greater government involvement across the board.

The American Party of the 1850s favored secrecy. It was nicknamed the "Know-Nothing Party" because,

NOTABLE THIRD PARTY & INDEPENDENT PRESIDENTIAL CANDIDATES

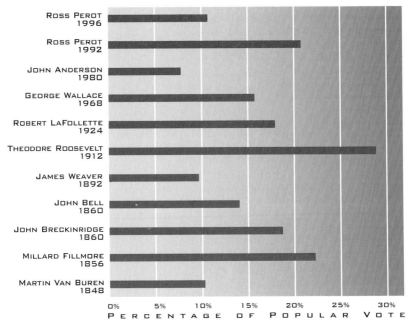

Data Sources: *1997 World Almanac & Book of Facts* (World Almanac Books, 1997) and "Presidential Elections Since 1789" (*Congressional Quarterly,* 5th ed., 1991).

when asked anything about the party, members replied "I don't know." The group opposed immigration, the Catholic Church, and the election or appointment of Roman Catholics and the foreign-born to government positions. The Know-Nothings split over the slavery issue and rapidly declined.[15]

Still other parties unite behind a specific candidate. In 1912 Theodore Roosevelt tried but failed to unite the conservative and progressive wings of the Republican Party. He and his supporters formed the Progressive Party, or "Bull Moose" Party, and Roosevelt ran for a third term as president, splitting the Republican vote.

Liberal Republican congressman John Anderson formed the National Unity Campaign to run for president in 1980. After running for president as an Independent in 1992, Ross Perot ran again in 1996 as the Reform Party candidate.[16]

A third party candidate has never won the presidency. Although third party victories are rare even at the state and local levels, Minnesotans elected Reform Party governor Jesse Ventura in 1998. Third party candidates also occasionally attract enough votes to affect the campaigns of major party candidates. If people who voted for Theodore Roosevelt on the Progressive Party ticket in 1912 had voted instead for Republican William Taft, the Democratic candidate, Woodrow Wilson, might not have been elected president.[17] Likewise,

*Minnesota governor Jesse Ventura takes the oath of office in 1998 as his wife, Terry, looks on.*

it's unclear whether Ross Perot's 1992 candidacy siphoned off votes that might otherwise have reelected Republican George Bush.

Can third parties make a difference? Former third party presidential candidate John Anderson said, "I agree that the role of the third party is to be the cutting edge, the leading edge, of the innovations that are needed to help us break out of the encrusted thinking that keeps us from really mounting an effective assault on our problems."[18]

## WHAT'S AHEAD?

Both Democrats and Republicans want to see their candidates elected. They also want to see their parties prosper and grow. But are the major parties becoming stronger or weaker?

A rise in "split-ticket voting"—voting for members of one party for some offices and another party for other offices—seems to confirm that a party label plays a smaller role in getting a candidate elected than it did fifty or one hundred years ago.[19] The once dominant role of political parties may also have declined due to a greater media emphasis on individual candidates and voter disenchantment.[20]

On the other hand, political science professors Stephen Ansolabehere of the Massachusetts Institute of Technology and Shanto Iyengar of the University of California Los Angeles suggest that disenchantment among middle-of-the-road voters leaves the real electoral power in the hands of a smaller number of committed party members. As the percentage heading to the polls shrinks, loyal party members may find their voices increasing.[21] In other words, extremists at both ends of the political spectrum gain influence as moderates abstain from voting.

Party affiliation plays an especially strong role in campaigns for the House of Representatives, where districts tend to traditionally vote either Democratic or Republican. From 1954 to 1992, fewer than 13 percent of the House seats switched party control from Democratic to Republican or vice versa.[22] This made the 1994 election of a majority of Republicans to Congress unusual. While Republicans still kept a majority in both houses, some traditionally Democratic seats reverted back in the 1996 and 1998 elections.

Political parties play a pivotal role in American campaigns. For most elections, choosing sides and being a "team player" is essential for anyone who wants to win.

*The first inauguration of President George Washington,*
*April 30, 1789*

# SCORING POINTS

What kind of person do you want leading the country, governing your state, or running your city? Practically everyone wants someone with "good character." Generally, this means someone who is honest, trustworthy, and intelligent. It means someone with leadership abilities, someone who commands respect and gets things done. Often, but not always, it also means someone who is active in the community and has a reasonably stable family life.

George Washington, the first president of the United States, was elected primarily on the basis of the strong character and leadership skills he had demonstrated during the Revolutionary War. Yet Washington insisted that the presidency held "no fascinating allurements for me," so he couldn't be accused of being "vain-glorious" and overly ambitious.[23]

History professor Gil Troy notes that during our country's early history, candidates "stood" for election, as opposed to actively running for office. As late as 1860, presidential candidate Stephen Douglas felt it was necessary to give excuses for traveling on the campaign trail. Instead of openly admitting that he was campaigning hard against Republican Abraham

*Stephen Douglas,* left, *ran for president against Abraham Lincoln in 1860.*

Lincoln, Douglas claimed he was just visiting his mother in upstate New York, attending his brother-in-law's graduation from Harvard in Massachusetts, and visiting his father's Connecticut gravesite.[24]

## KEEPING UP APPEARANCES

The political arena has changed dramatically since then. Turn on the television, read any newspaper or national news magazine, and you're almost certain to see news of candidates running for public office. In the age of mass media, candidates have learned just how important it is to keep up appearances.

In 1960 voters sat riveted to their black and white televisions to see Republican candidate Richard Nixon face off against Democratic candidate John Kennedy in the first series of televised presidential debates. Both men initially resisted the makeup crew. Finally, Kennedy accepted makeup around his eyes, and Nixon wore "Lazy Shave" powder to cover his "five o'clock" beard shadow.

During the debate, Kennedy came across as intelligent, confident, and attractive. Nixon, in contrast, seemed slouched, strained, and uncertain. The candidates' behavior on camera clearly influenced the voters. When election day came, Kennedy won.[25]

Twenty-eight years later, in 1988, staff for Democratic presidential candidate Michael Dukakis requested— and got—a platform for the Massachusetts governor to stand on during televised debates with his taller opponent, Republican George H. W. Bush. That way, both candidates appeared equal in stature and, presumably, in leadership ability.

Candidates' staffs advise them how to dress and act on television. Men often sport a dark suit with a pale gray shirt. Women dress conservatively, without flowery prints or ruffles. With few exceptions, however, politicians are not polished actors, and even a small foible can send the wrong message to a television audience. In 1992, for example, George Bush's supporters inwardly groaned when the incumbent president glanced at his watch during one of the presidential

*Presidential candidates George Bush, left, and Michael Dukakis, right, before the start of their debate at Wake Forest University in Winston-Salem, North Carolina, September 25, 1988*

debates. The small gesture came across as suggesting that the president was bored with the debate.

Carefully coached candidates look for opportunities other than formal debates to appear on television and radio. In 1992, for example, both major party candidates, George Bush and Bill Clinton, and Reform Party candidate Ross Perot appeared separately as guests on CNN's *Larry King Live.* Other appearances are more whimsical, such as John Kennedy joking on the *Tonight Show* in 1960, Richard Nixon appearing on *Laugh-In* in 1968, and Bill Clinton playing the saxophone on Arsenio Hall's late night show in 1992.[26]

Certainly not all politicians are handsome or beautiful, but successful campaigners usually have to present a polished appearance during speeches, public events, and television broadcasts. The more confident a candidate appears, the more points he or she seems to score with the voters.

## INCUMBENCY—THE ADDED EDGE

Statistically speaking, the easiest way to win an election is to already hold office. Incumbents, or current officeholders, who seek reelection tend to win 90 percent of the time.[27] Name recognition is important, and incumbents are known to the public from their previous campaigns. When current officeholders take significant actions or make public appearances, they continually get their names in the news. Newsletters or other publicly funded communications also reinforce the message that Jane or John Legislator is helping the people back home. Incumbents can also capitalize on their experience. By highlighting the accomplishments of their last term, incumbents' campaign speeches deliver the clear message that they are, once again, the best men and women for the job.[28]

While challengers assemble campaign staffs from scratch, incumbents have the benefit of a prior campaign organization. Some legitimate office staff functions, such as preparing position papers on pending legislative issues, gauging voter sentiment from letters, e-mail, and phone calls, and coordinating the candidate's schedule, can significantly aid the reelection effort.

Incumbents also find it easier to raise campaign funds. Since 1980 more than 60 percent of money from political action committees (PACs) has gone to incumbents seeking reelection, rather than to challengers or candidates for open seats.[29] PACs raise money from groups of people to support candidates and election issues that are consistent with the groups' goals. Incumbents are also well situated to make connections with people and organizations able to contribute funds for reelection.

**TAKING A STAND**

Most voters want their elected representatives not only to be honest but also to express their views on important policy issues and to take action that is consistent with those views. During any political campaign, "hot-button" issues—topics that evoke strong emotional reaction among voters—depend in large part on the particular moment in history.

In the mid-nineteenth century, slavery was the major issue. Strong antislavery support from the North elected Republican Abraham Lincoln in 1860. That hot-button issue set the stage for the Civil War.

Economic well-being—or lack thereof—is a recurring campaign theme. In 1932, during the Great Depression, Democrat Franklin D. Roosevelt campaigned for the presidency against Republican Herbert Hoover. Unemployment ran as high as 25 percent, and poverty was rampant. Promising "a new deal for the American people," Roosevelt easily won his first term as president.[30] He established the Civilian Conservation Corps (CCC), which gave work and training to 2.5 million young people. He set up the Works Projects Administration (WPA), which employed an additional 2 million people. He also established Social Security and other programs aimed at reducing economic suffering.

*Franklin Delano Roosevelt gave hope to impoverished Americans during the Great Depression.*

Civil rights and equal opportunities for all Americans were hot-button issues in the late 1950s and the 1960s. Participants in frequent civil rights demonstrations demanded equality for people of color. Also, the United States faced pockets of severe poverty. Lyndon Johnson's 1964 presidential campaign promised to build a Great Society in which government involvement would overcome these problems. In sharp contrast, George Wallace's 1968 American Independent Party campaign appealed to groups who resisted civil rights reforms and social welfare programs.[31]

Economic prosperity resurfaced as a hot-button issue in the 1980s. In 1980 and 1984, about 30 percent of all commercials in the presidential campaign related to the economy.[32] In 1980 Ronald Reagan charged that President Jimmy Carter had failed to deal effectively with inflation and unemployment. Reagan, in turn, promised to balance the budget, cut taxes, and increase defense spending—all at the same time—and he won by a large margin. When Reagan was up for reelection in 1984, Democratic challenger and former vice president Walter Mondale warned that the growing federal budget deficit would erode America's economic well-being. In response, Ronald Reagan's "Morning in America" ads celebrated the country's economic growth during his first term in office. The mellow ads featured people expressing renewed pride in being Americans and thanks for the prosperity they enjoyed under Reagan's leadership.

Related to general economic issues is the question of taxes. During his 1988 presidential campaign against Michael Dukakis, Republican George Bush had pledged not to raise taxes if he was elected president. "Read my lips," he had said. "No new taxes."[33] He won the presidential election, but then he approved a tax increase, breaking his personal pledge to the American people. When Bush was campaigning for reelection in 1992, many people felt he had betrayed them and voted instead for Democrat Bill Clinton or Reform Party candidate Ross Perot.

When a recession occurred in the early 1990s, the economy again became a primary issue. During the 1992 presidential campaign, the candidates differed on questions about balancing the budget, the mounting federal debt, the creation of new jobs, the future of Social Security, and other major financial obligations. Although the candidates disagreed about solutions to those problems, their basic message to voters was the same: Vote for me, and I will improve the standard of living for the American people.

Another issue that came to the forefront in 1992 was "family values." Running for reelection in 1992, Republican Vice President Dan Quayle lamented the decreasing number of traditional families with two married parents. He viewed nontraditional families with single parents, divorced parents, or homosexual parents as less desirable and as a threat to traditional values.

The Democrats had their own ideas about the family values issue. The 1992 Clinton campaign argued that all families—traditional and nontraditional—should have adequate resources to provide a safe, healthy, and supportive atmosphere for their children. Where resources were lacking, government assistance programs could make up the difference. The phrase "family values" clearly meant different things to the opposing political camps.

America's changing social, economic, and international roles will define the hot-button issues of the future. What candidates say and how voters react to those issues will determine who governs the United States in the coming decades.

## BEYOND OUR BORDERS

Throughout the twentieth century, foreign policy played a leading role in national elections. After World War I, Americans became wrapped in a wave of isolationist sentiment. Senators reflected public opinion when they rejected the 1919 Treaty of Versailles and U.S. membership in the League of Nations. After World War I, Americans were tired of fighting what they viewed as European battles and feared that the League would involve further entanglements in European disputes. Promising a "return to normalcy," Republican Warren Harding handily won the 1920 presidential election.

The United States' withdrawal from world affairs ended abruptly on December 7, 1941, when the Japanese bombed the U.S. naval base at Pearl Harbor in Hawaii. Suddenly the country found itself fighting World War II on two fronts—in the Pacific against the Japanese and in Europe against the Nazis. With the war still going on in 1944, the Democratic Party urged voters not to change leadership midstream. Voters agreed, electing Franklin Roosevelt to an unprecedented fourth term as president.

Foreign policy again dominated national elections in the late 1960s, when many Americans opposed U.S.

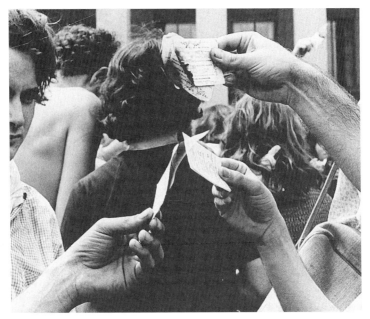

*On May 22, 1972, antiwar demonstrators in Washington, D.C., burn their draft cards on the steps of the Pentagon to protest the Vietnam War.*

involvement in the Vietnam War. Democratic president Lyndon Johnson ordered the first U.S. combat troops into South Vietnam and increased bombing attacks. The evening news broadcast vivid scenes from the battlefront, bringing the horrors of war directly into American living rooms. As the "honor roll" of young people killed in the conflict grew longer, protests against the draft and the war became louder and more violent.

In 1968 Senator Eugene McCarthy of Minnesota, one of President Johnson's own party members, led the antiwar movement by challenging Johnson for the Democratic presidential nomination. Although McCarthy did not win the nomination, President Johnson decided not to run for a second term. After a bitter, raucous convention, Vice President Hubert Humphrey got his party's nomination, but Republican Richard Nixon won the election.[34] The following year, the United States began to reduce its forces in Vietnam.

## BUILDING BRIDGES

Every public issue at the local and national level offers candidates a chance to score points by picking up votes among people who agree with their positions. Of course, different voters place priorities on different issues. Each group of voters with similar interests forms a constituency.

For example, elderly people form one constituency. Among other things, they are concerned about Social Security payments, Medicare, and the availability of resources for older people. Parents in their 30s and 40s are another constituency. They are often concerned about high taxes and educational opportunities for their children.

In order to win a majority of votes, successful candidates need to appeal to as many constituencies as possible. This can be a delicate balancing act, especially when the needs of one group potentially conflict with those of another. In 1999, for example, the federal government predicted the first budget surplus in decades. Immediately, people weighed in with ideas on how to spend the surplus.

Vice President Al Gore, aiming for the Democratic presidential nomination in 2000, said the surplus should be used for Social Security, Medicare benefits, and educational improvements.[35] Those ideas appeal to

*Demonstrators demand
the protection of Social
Security and Medicare
benefits.*

the elderly and some other groups, but they conflict
with the interests of high-wage earners, who would
benefit from a Republican-sponsored tax cut.[36] Still another choice would be to spend any surplus on govern-
ment-sponsored research and development. This would
be popular with people at universities and in the high-
tech sector.[37] Yet that option would leave both the social
benefits camp and the tax cut camp dissatisfied.

Candidates hope the combination of their positions
on the issues will appeal to the greatest number of
voters. While campaigning for general principles of a
better economy, safer streets, or better health care, candidates often fail to discuss exactly how they propose to
achieve their goals until after the election. Avoiding
specifics means risking fewer broken campaign
promises after the election.

Gender plays a role too. One 1996 survey showed men preferred Republican candidates to Democrats by a ratio of approximately 5 to 4. In contrast, women backed Democrats over Republicans by a ratio of about 2 to 1.[38] This gender gap grew steadily in the 1990s, and the enormous voting potential held by women had both Democrats and Republicans clamoring for women's votes.[39]

Of course, every candidate would love to have the ardent support of every voter, but the bottom line in campaign politics is winning the most votes. If a candidate can convince enough people to vote for her or him over the opponent—even if the preference is just a slight one—then the election race will be won.

*Al Gore smiles confidently while answering reporters' questions in Hanover, New Hampshire, October 22, 1999.*

*George W. Bush on the 2000 presidential campaign trail*

# CALLING THE SHOTS

During the first 150 years of the country's history, American voters relied largely on newspapers, magazines, pamphlets, and circulars to learn about candidates and where they stood on the issues. Radio broadcasting since the mid-1920s and television since the 1950s have played a major role in campaign politics. Voters can hear and see the candidates and quickly learn about their positions on specific issues.

Media coverage not only reports on campaign politics but also influences how candidates conduct their campaigns. With the Internet providing voters with a new window on the world, the media seems poised to play an even bigger role.

### SLOGANS AND SOUND BITES

A half-hour television news program has only about 22 minutes in which to cover national and world news. Although there isn't enough time to present a detailed description of election issues, networks do want to report on developments in various campaigns. Instead of providing a long, detailed analysis of each candidate's positions, news writers scan the candidates' speeches

51

for sound bites. Sound bites are brief statements—usually 12 seconds or less—that summarize a candidate's bottom-line position on an issue.

Aware that newscasters will probably show only a brief sound bite from a 30-minute speech, a candidate's speech writers pepper the presentation with punchy statements. They want not only to convey their candidate's position on an issue but also to make television viewers at home sit up and take notice. In this way, the sound bite becomes the message transmitted to the voter.

On the one hand, sound bites communicate the broad-brush outlines of a candidate's policy position. Paid ad time is costly, but sound bites get the candidate prime-time coverage in news media that would not cover an in-depth discussion of the issues. Sound bites also communicate in language that voters identify with.

On the other hand, sound bites oversimplify policy issues and often appeal to emotion rather than reason. Combined with catchy campaign slogans and slick advertising, the sound bite mentality discourages thoughtful analysis of complex questions. Political communication through the mass media begins to resemble ads for fast food, toilet paper, and headache medicine.

## IS ALL THE NEWS FIT TO PRINT?

The banner of the *New York Times* bears the slogan, "All the News That's Fit to Print." Journalists pride themselves on presenting the news in an informed, impartial way, but does campaign reporting sometimes slip over the "fitness" line? Or does freedom of the press mean that the public has a right to know anything and everything about the people who run for office?

In the early part of the twentieth century, reporters had a tacit understanding that they would avoid stories about politicians' personal shortcomings. For example, even though presidents Franklin Roosevelt and John Kennedy were rumored to be unfaithful to their wives, the traditional press consciously refrained from reporting such stories.[40]

By the late twentieth century, however, the media had developed a much more open attitude about discussing sexual affairs and other previously taboo issues. And reporters reacted swiftly to any perceived challenge from politicians about the completeness or accuracy of their reporting.

In May 1987, Senator Gary Hart, a Colorado Democrat, was almost certain to be his party's choice for the 1988 presidential nomination. Then rumors surfaced that Hart was unfaithful to his wife, Lee. When Hart adamantly denied the rumors, reporters for the *Miami Herald* snapped pictures of the 50-year-old politician cuddling with a 29-year-old actress on the yacht *Monkey Business*. The story made national news. If Hart couldn't be trusted to be faithful to his wife, could he be trusted to lead the United States and keep his

**Democrat Gary Hart speaks at a U.S. Senate committee meeting in Washington, D.C., in the early 1980s.**

campaign promises? After enough newspapers raised these questions, Hart withdrew from the campaign.

Rather than apologize for his earlier dishonesty in denying the affair, Hart blamed the press for destroying his chances for the presidency. "If someone's able to throw up a smoke screen and keep it there long enough," he said, "you can't get your message across. You can't raise the money to finance a campaign, there's too much static, and you can't communicate."[41]

Many stories have made juicy reading: an exotic dancer diving into the Washington, D.C., Tidal Basin from a senator's car; a congressman becoming romantically involved with a typist who couldn't type; a conservative Maryland politician arrested on charges of soliciting a male prostitute; a senator attacked in the press for being publicly drunk.[42] The resulting political fallout stems not only from the public's disapproval of the elected officials' behavior, but also from their poor judgment and arrogance in acting as if they were above the law.[43]

Not all stories are true, however. Reports of alleged cocaine use almost destroyed the career of former White House chief of staff Hamilton Jordan. Jordan's career was salvaged only after the charges were proved false.[44] When media stories like that are published about candidates on the campaign trail, they can cause significant emotional distress to the person involved and loss of esteem among voters—even if charges later turn out to be untrue.

Supreme Court decisions hold that the news media cannot be held liable for damages caused to public figures, such as politicians, unless a person proves both that the story was false and that it was published with malicious intent.[45] Otherwise, the prospect of civil liability would have a chilling effect upon the freedom of the press guaranteed by the First Amendment to the Constitution.

Having stepped into the public limelight, should politicians just accept that their lives are fair game for scrutiny by the press and the American public? If allegations in a story are false, is a small correction notice sufficient to correct the damage, or should a sense of fair play lead the media to give just as much attention to publicizing their error as they did to the original story? How can voters detect which private issues might affect a candidate's ability to govern and which incidents are irrelevant?

## A HORSE RACE?

"Where Clinton Leads by a Mile—And Where It's Close."[46]

"Why Bob Dole Is Stuck in a Rut."[47]

"Dole Must Close 'Gender Gap' to Avoid Clinton Landslide."[48]

These and other media stories focus on the "horse race" aspects of elections—which candidates are ahead, which candidates are neck and neck, and which are falling behind. Surveying groups of people all across the country, professional pollsters analyze how politicians rate with different segments of the population—men, women, whites, blacks, college-educated, blue-collar workers, and so on. Technically speaking, polls provide a snapshot of public opinion: If the election were held right now, how would you vote? Polls provide helpful information for campaign managers about how a candidate is perceived by specific groups of voters at a specific point in the campaign. Meanwhile, the news media report the results of the polls, creating news out of the political race itself.

Using up-to-date statistical sampling methods, polls can come remarkably close to predicting the election outcomes. Polls have correctly predicted the winner in every presidential election since 1950. For example, in 1984 the Gallup Poll correctly predicted that incumbent Republican president Ronald Reagan would beat Democratic challenger Walter Mondale by a popular vote of 59 percent to 41 percent.[49]

But polls are not perfect. Perhaps the biggest gaffe occurred in 1948, when the Gallup Poll predicted that Republican Thomas Dewey would beat President Harry Truman, the Democratic candidate, by five percentage points. The *Chicago Tribune* printed its early edition for the morning after election day with the headline, "DEWEY DEFEATS TRUMAN." In fact, when the ballots from November 2, 1948, were counted, Truman had beaten Dewey by 4.5 percentage points.[50]

*Harry Truman laughs over the headline "DEWEY DEFEATS TRUMAN."*

Election polls are still imperfect. Although the bottom-line prediction was correct, the last poll taken by CBS News and the *New York Times* before the 1996 election predicted that Democrat Bill Clinton would win a second term by 18 percentage points. Other polls by Harris, NBC, ABC, and CNN predicted Clinton would have a 12 to 23 percent margin of victory. In fact, Clinton won by only 8 percentage points—a victory, but hardly the predicted landslide.[51]

Political science professors Robert Erikson of the University of Houston and Lee Sigelman of George Washington University analyzed 227 polls of midterm congressional elections from 1950 through 1994. They compared the polls' predictions with what actually happened in elections. The polls erred by up to 7 percentage points. Most polls predicted higher percentages of votes for Democratic candidates than were actually cast.[52]

Erikson and Sigelman called this effect a pro-Democratic bias. They suggested that more people may identify with the Democratic Party in principle and tell pollsters they support the Democratic candidate, even if they don't know much about the individual running for office.[53] A different explanation, however, is the possibility that polls influence voter turnout.

When pollsters turn in predictions, people may sense that the outcome of the election is a foregone conclusion. As the 1996 polls predicted Clinton would win by a landslide, voter turnout at the polls dropped to its lowest rate for a presidential election since 1924.[54] Did Dole supporters decide that their vote wouldn't make any difference? Or did voters in the Clinton camp conclude that they didn't need to take the time to vote because the result was a foregone conclusion?

Speaking at a National Press Club luncheon the day after the 1996 presidential election, Dan Hazelwood, a political consultant for the defeated Bob Dole, sharply criticized journalists for failing to focus on the issues and misinterpreting public opinion polls. "If you eliminate the ability of journalists to cite poll numbers in their stories, they wouldn't have anything to write about," Hazelwood argued.[55]

Mark Mellman, who has served as a pollster for various Democratic candidates, agrees that incorrect interpretation of polls can adversely affect elections. After a poll was published showing Mellman's client Lydia Spottswood to be more than 20 percentage points behind Republican Mark Neumann in a Wisconsin congressional race, funding support for Spottswood's campaign dried up "significantly." With Neumann winning by only two thousand votes, Mellman questions whether release of the poll influenced not just campaign financing but also the way people voted on election day.[56]

Exit polls present other problems. Exit polls survey voters just after they've cast their ballots on election day. Radio and television networks have used exit polls to predict the victorious candidates—even before election officials have counted all the actual votes. Some stations wait voluntarily until polls close in a state. Then they make predictions based on exit polls plus a small percentage of counted votes.

While this practice is just quick reporting for state and local races, it is controversial in presidential elections. Broadcasters may declare a winner even before voting ends in western states, where the time zone makes it three to six hours later than in the eastern states. "And that's an abuse of the exit polls," claims Curtis Gans of the Committee for the Study of the American Electorate.[57]

Reporters defend their right to report poll results and to make predictions based on all data available to them. "That's what people want to know about," argues newscaster Tom Brokaw.[58] Likewise, many pollsters say that campaign managers, the media, and the public have a right to know where people rank during the course of a campaign. Some analysts, such as political communication professors Doris Graber and Steven Chaffee, even argue that accurate polling can give a better sense of how the population as a whole feels than election results can. After all, election day results depend on who shows up to vote.[59]

According to the Constitution and our country's laws, however, the vote on election day is the only poll that really counts for deciding who will hold public office. Ideally, people's votes should be based on their views of the candidates and the issues rather than on who seems to be leading in the race. As a practical matter, however, the news media will continue to publish poll results, and the First Amendment protects their legal right to do so. Ultimately, the decision of whether and how much to rely upon polling results lies with the individual voter.

*President Lyndon B. Johnson was the thirty-sixth president of the United States.*

# HITTING BELOW THE BELT

The little girl plucking daisies counted, "1, 2, 3, 4, 5. . . . " Meanwhile, a voice-over announcer counted too: "10, 9, 8, 7, 6, 5, 4, 3, 2, 1." At the end of his countdown, the scene disintegrated into the mushroom cloud of an atomic bomb explosion. Then came the voice of President Lyndon Johnson: "These are the stakes. To make a world in which all of God's children can live, or to go into the dark. We must either love each other, or we must die."[60]

Aired during NBC's *Monday Night at the Movies* on September 7, 1964, the Daisy ad captured more attention than the feature film. Johnson's opponent, Republican senator Barry Goldwater, was a political conservative who supported a strong military. By striking at voters' horror of nuclear holocaust, the Daisy ad drew a sharp distinction between the two candidates. The next night, each network's nightly news replayed the Daisy ad and its powerful imagery. Millions more voters experienced the fear of nuclear destruction evoked by the ad.

Because of the controversy, the Johnson campaign pulled the ad and didn't pay to show it again. Thanks to the boost from network news coverage of the commercial, viewers got the message. Other issues helped Johnson win the election, including his incumbency after President Kennedy's assassination and his commitment to work for social programs that the late president had called for. However, the Daisy ad effectively contrasted a dovish president to his hawkish opponent—despite Johnson's support of the ongoing Vietnam conflict.[61]

## THE REVOLVING DOOR CAMPAIGN

By the summer of 1988, Democratic opponent Governor Michael Dukakis of Massachusetts was running neck and neck in the polls with Republican George Bush in the presidential campaign. Finally, Bush supporters settled on a campaign theme—the "revolving door" of prisons—that struck fear in the hearts of Americans. A high percentage of convicted criminals are repeat offenders. Just as an office building's revolving doors spin around and around as people enter and leave, Bush's campaign advisers said prisons, too, have revolving doors. The Bush ads implied that prisons released criminals back onto the streets only to have them commit more crimes and return again.

Central to this theme was Willie Horton—a black man sentenced to life in prison for murder. Massachusetts, however, had a program that allowed furloughs—temporary stays outside the prison. Horton escaped while he was out on one of those furloughs. Before he could be recaptured, Horton kidnapped a man and a woman. He stabbed the man and brutally raped the woman.

Playing on the crime's national headlines, Bush

declared he would be tough on crime. While ads directly sponsored by Bush's campaign didn't mention Horton by name, they broadcast powerful images such as the revolving prison door. Voters couldn't help but associate the ads with Horton.

A television ad sponsored by the National Security Political Action Committee was even less subtle. Aiming to turn public opinion against the Democratic candidate, it claimed: "Dukakis not only opposes the death penalty, he allowed first degree murderers to have weekend passes from prison. One was Willie Horton, who murdered a boy in a robbery, stabbing him 19 times. Despite a life sentence, Horton received 10 weekend passes from prison. Horton fled, kidnapped a young couple, stabbing the man and repeatedly raping his girlfriend."[62]

The implication was clear. A vote for Dukakis would be a vote for crime and violence, while a vote for Bush would support safety and security.

The ad did more than just evoke a strong emotional response. Political science professors Stephen Ansolabehere and Shanto Iyengar believe the Revolving Door ad was also factually misleading. It gave the impression that many people in the prison's furlough program committed violent crimes, instead of just Horton. Moreover, the ads implied that Dukakis designed the prison furlough program, when it was actually set up by the Republican governor who preceded him.[63]

By highlighting a crime by a black man against a white woman, the Revolving Door ad also appealed to racial prejudices and stereotypes. "The symbolism was very powerful," commented Dukakis's campaign manager, law professor Susan Estrich. "You can't find a stronger metaphor, intended or not, for racial hatred in this country than a black man raping a white woman."[64]

Was the Revolving Door theme a fair dramatization of the differences between the two candidates' positions on the death penalty and the prison system? Or was it a misleading appeal to fear and prejudice? In either case, the Revolving Door ad had its desired effect. Bush surged ahead of Dukakis in the polls and won the election.

## NOTHING NEW

The Daisy and Revolving Door ads are two examples of negative campaigning. Rather than focusing positively on the strengths of one candidate, they emphasize perceived negative aspects of the opponent. Instead of urging people to vote *for* one candidate, they encourage voters to cast their ballots *against* the other.

Negative campaigning is nothing new. In the election campaigns of 1796 and 1800, Federalist supporters of John Adams called opponent Thomas Jefferson a swindler, an atheist, and a traitor. They even accused Jefferson of raping a slave woman.[65]

Jefferson's supporters, in turn, branded Adams an egotist, a monarchist, and a traitor. In an essay called "The Prospect Before Us," Democratic-Republican James Callender wrote, "[T]his federal gem John Adams, this apostle of the parsons of Connecticut, is not only a repulsive pedant [educated show-off], a gross hypocrite, and an unprincipled oppressor, but that he is, in private life, one of the most egregious fools upon the continent."[66] Despite the accusations, both men won turns at the presidency and a revered place in American history.

During the 1840 presidential campaign, attackers called Whig Party nominee William Henry Harrison "General Mum." They claimed he was an old "imbecile" and a "caged" simpleton. "I am the most persecuted and calumniated [slandered] individual now living," complained Harrison.[67]

## WHAT'S SO WRONG?

Why all the fuss about negative campaigning? After all, don't voters have a right to know all the pros and cons about the candidates? Since candidates aren't likely to advertise their shortcomings, isn't it up to their opponents to point them out?

In the 1996 congressional campaign, Democratic candidate Dennis Kucinich's ads never mentioned that he had been mayor of Cleveland when the city defaulted on its loan obligations in 1977. Since Congress is responsible for the entire federal budget, his Republican opponent, Martin Hoke, felt this history reflected poorly on Kucinich's ability to manage finances. Using a theme of "wrong then, wrong now," political commercials reminded viewers about the city's loan default.[68] Were the ads a personal attack or a legitimate contrast between the candidates' experiences and qualifications?

Ideally, people prefer to vote *for* a candidate rather than *against* that person's opponent. Barraged by negative campaigns, voters may feel their election choice is to pick the lesser of two evils.

Reliability is another problem. Generally speaking, a person who falsely accuses another person of committing a crime or immoral act can be held liable in court to pay damages for harming the other person's reputation. But it is harder to win a claim of slander or libel when the person involved is a public figure. As a result, the news media and political opponents can make statements more freely than they might if they were speaking about a private individual.

Moreover, many "statements" in negative ads are vague and general. The Revolving Door ads, for example, never said Governor Dukakis instituted the prison furlough program or that he in any way approved of Willie Horton's violent actions. Yet those were the unspoken and misleading implications.

When political campaigns become mudslinging matches, the name-calling draws voters' attention away from policy issues. Rather than voting to make a positive change in public policy, voters cast their ballots based on impressions left from negative campaign ads. Instead of focusing on needed changes in the economy, foreign policy, social welfare, or defense, voters may focus on scandal or personal foibles.

Sometimes negative campaigning can backfire. The 1998 New York Senate race between Republican incumbent Al D'Amato and Democratic candidate Charles Schumer was nasty on both sides. Both candidates used name-calling and mudslinging. Then D'Amato called Schumer a "putzhead"—an offensive Yiddish insult. No one knows for sure how much the final vote was affected by voters who felt insulted by the crass remark, but media perception seemed to shift in favor of Schumer, who ultimately won the election.[69]

Also in 1998, President Bill Clinton was tried on

*Gary Hoover and his daughter, Bobbi Jo, of Clarksburg, Virginia, were among two thousand people who rallied to support President Bill Clinton on the day scheduled for the impeachment vote, December 17, 1998.*

impeachment charges for alleged failure to disclose full information in sworn testimony about his former relationship with a White House intern. In the fall congressional campaigns, some Republican ads tried to link Democratic opponents to the president.[70] The Republicans' failure to increase their overall majority in the House and Senate suggests that the strategy backfired.

Negative campaigns can also cause voters to become frustrated with the political system. Instead of going to the polls to vote for the candidate of their choice, voters may stay home and vote for "none of the above." After conducting a four-year study of negative campaign ads, Stephen Ansolabehere and Shanto Iyengar contend that negative ads actually shrink the electorate by causing voters in the political "middle" to become frustrated and disenchanted. In turn, political party loyalists whose views are reinforced by negative campaigning may acquire a disproportionate voice in selecting the country's leaders.[71]

## NOT ABOUT TO STOP

"People say they hate negative advertising, but it works," says Democratic consultant Jill Buckley.[72]

Republican media adviser Janet Mullins, who worked on President Bush's 1988 campaign, agrees. "Everybody hates negative ads," she says, "then they rate them most effective in terms of decision making."[73]

Politicians recognize the effectiveness of negative campaign ads too. "They're winning all over," New Jersey senator Frank Lautenberg complained. "People like them, the same way that they like wrestling and violence in the movies."[74] By touching on topics that grab voters' attention, negative campaign ads become memorable. And the more memorable an ad is—even if viewers don't like it—the more likely it is that the ad will factor into their voting choice.

### RESPONDING TO ATTACKS

Candidates faced with negative campaigning rarely tolerate the attacks in silence. In the world of political mudslinging, this would be seen as admitting the worst claims of an opponent. So candidates use different strategies to fend off attacks.

One approach is to take the high road and avoid making negative attacks against an opponent. As Congressional Representative Morris Udall once said, "In my own campaigns I try to heed the wise old Navaho adage, 'He who slings mud loses ground.'"[75] If the opponent then begins an attack campaign, the candidate can point to his or her own spotless record of playing fair.

Another approach is to preempt an anticipated attack. Americans had never elected a Catholic president before 1960. Indeed, when New York governor Al Smith, who was Catholic, ran for president in 1928, prejudiced people argued that Catholics' allegiance to the pope as head of the church might interfere with their patriotic duties. To ward off potential attacks motivated by that prejudice, Democrat John Kennedy not only confirmed his loyalty to the United States, but he promised to work to combat other forms of bigotry too.[76]

Deflection is another strategy. In 1992 Bill Clinton might have floundered in the Democratic primaries after a nightclub singer claimed she had had a twelve-year affair with him. Appearing with his wife, Hillary, on the highly ranked television show *60 Minutes,* Clinton admitted there had been some past "wrongdoing" in his marriage, but he reaffirmed his commitment to his wife and to his country. "I think the American people who saw that *60 Minutes* program saw two people who love each other and respect each other and are very proud they didn't give up on their marriage," Clinton said afterward.[77]

Yet another strategy is the counterattack. A vigorous example is the Torricelli ads against opponent Dick Zimmer described in the first chapter of this book. Indeed, with the "no holds barred" attitude surrounding political campaigns, candidates shouldn't venture into attack ads unless they are ready and willing to defend themselves against even more aggressive counterattacks.

Beyond the candidates' responses, the most important question is how voters respond to negative campaigning. What is your opinion of negative campaign ads? How, if at all, would you let campaign tactics influence your voting decisions on election day?

*President Nixon's involvement with improper campaign fund-raising led to strict laws on campaign contributions.*

# PAY TO PLAY?

Vice President Al Gore said he thought the April 1996 luncheon at the Hsi Lai Buddhist Temple in Hacienda Heights, California, was a "community event." Regular community events, however, don't raise $140,000 for the Democratic National Committee and give the appearance that a tax-exempt institution might endorse a political party. Moreover, several $5,000 contributions supposedly came from monks and nuns who had taken vows of poverty. Probing showed the money really came from foreign sources that were legally prohibited from making campaign contributions.

After the incident made national headlines, the Democratic National Committee reimbursed the temple $15,000 for the costs of the program and gave back some donations. The party also suspended John Huang, the Democratic Party official who arranged the fund-raiser. By then, significant questions had been raised about how much, if anything, Vice President Gore knew before attending the temple event.[78]

Other scandals plagued the 1996 Clinton-Gore re-election campaign too. Although foreign citizens are legally prohibited from contributing to federal campaigns in the United States, allegations surfaced that Indonesian business magnate Mochtar Riady and his family had funneled $1.2 million to the Democratic Party since 1991.[79]

Then there were eyebrow-raising "sleepovers." The Democratic National Committee arranged for certain top donors to Clinton's reelection campaign to spend a night in the Lincoln Bedroom, a historic room that President Lincoln used when he lived in the White House. Were the invitations a way for the president to get reacquainted with good friends? Or was the access to the president, provided by the invitations, a payment for campaign donations?[80]

Republicans had hassles too. In December 1996, Newt Gingrich, Speaker of the House of Representatives, admitted that he had failed to seek and follow legal advice that would have prevented improper money transfers from tax-exempt organizations to a political action committee. Gingrich also admitted that "inaccurate, incomplete, and unreliable statements were given" to the House Ethics Committee investigating

*Republican Newt Gingrich, Speaker of the House of Representatives, in 1996*

campaign abuses. The House fined Gingrich $300,000 for his violations.[81]

Why do so many problems revolve around campaign fund-raising? And what is all that money used for anyway? Is it possible for a candidate to win an election without spending lots of money?

### POLITICIANS IN THEIR POCKETS?

The more resources a campaign has, the better it can get its message out, urging people to vote for one candidate over another. The U.S. Supreme Court has recognized the citizens' right to donate campaign funds as a form of political speech protected under the First Amendment.[82] But when is the line crossed between free speech and bribery?

In the nineteenth century, large businesses shamelessly contributed huge amounts of money to political campaigns. In 1896, for example, Republican presidential candidate William McKinley received millions of dollars from banks, life insurance companies, petroleum companies, and other businesses that hoped for favorable government treatment.[83]

Investigative reporters who discovered and wrote about these and other abuses by public officials were called "muckrakers." Their reports led to public outcry. Elected representatives were supposed to represent all the people, not just a few wealthy individuals, businesses, or special interest groups.

Between 1907 and 1947, Congress tried to address the problems. The 1907 Tillman Act said national banks and corporations could not directly give money to federal campaigns.[84] The Federal Corrupt Practices

Act of 1925 required disclosure of contributions and imposed spending limits on candidates' election committees, but the limits were meaningless. Not only could candidates have as many election committees as they wanted, but the law was rarely enforced.[85] The 1939 Hatch Act prohibited federal employees from taking an active part in political campaigns.[86]

The Federal Election Campaign Act of 1971 contained much stricter provisions. For example, candidates in federal elections could not spend more than 10¢ per member of the voting age population or $50,000 (whichever was greater) for communications media. Only 60 percent of that amount could be spent on broadcast stations.[87] Presidential candidates could not spend more than $50,000 of their own money on an election.[88] And candidates and campaign committees had to fully report their fund-raising.[89]

But enforcement was left to the Justice Department, whose leaders were appointed by the president. Although 7,100 cases were referred to the Justice Department after Republican Richard Nixon's defeat of Democrat George McGovern in 1972, few cases were actually prosecuted.[90] When the public finally learned about the abuses, people were outraged.

Not only did the Republicans' Committee to Reelect the President (CRP) maintain a huge slush fund of unreported donations, but it also used that money to finance a 1972 break-in of Democratic campaign headquarters in Washington's Watergate office complex. Besides uncovering CRP's "dirty tricks" and spy tactics, a lawsuit by Common Cause—a nonprofit consumer group—and investigative reporting by *Washington Post* correspondents Bob Woodward and Carl Bernstein revealed huge, unreported "fat cat" donations to CRP. Millionaire Howard Hughes gave $100,000 in cash. Banking and oil heir Richard Scaife gave $1 million. Chicago insurance executive W. Clement Stone donated $2 million. When tape recordings revealed that Nixon agreed to help cover up the Watergate break-in, Congressional representatives started considering impeachment proceedings. On August 9, 1974, Nixon resigned from office.[91]

To prevent such abuses from happening again, Congress passed the Federal Election Campaign Act Amendments of 1974.[92] The law established the Federal Election Commission as an independent enforcement agency. The statute has since been amended several times. In 1976 Congress revised the statute to comply with the Supreme Court's ruling on the law's constitutionality in *Buckley v. Valeo.*[93] Those changes limited individual contributions to national parties to $20,000 per year and individual contributions to a PAC to $5,000 per year. Other amendments from 1979 through 1996 updated and streamlined the law but did

**Washington Post reporters Carl Bernstein, left, *and Bob Woodward,* right, *led the investigation of the Watergate scandal. Their reporting won a Pulitzer Prize in 1973.***

not change its fundamental structure.[94] As of early 2000, federal law limits the amount any individual may donate to a candidate to $1,000 per election, with a total of $25,000 during any calendar year. Foreign nationals may not make any contributions to candidates for federal office.

Corporations and labor unions are prohibited from making direct contributions to federal candidates. However, people within those organizations can donate voluntarily to a political action committee. The PAC, in turn, can make donations of $5,000 per candidate, per election. To ensure that limitations are obeyed, and to let the public know which interests support particular candidates, candidates must file timely reports with the Federal Election Commission.[95]

Additionally, federal law provides for limited public funding of presidential campaigns. A check-off box on federal income tax returns lets individuals designate three dollars of their tax money for this fund. Besides paying major party convention expenses, the money supplements major party candidates' private fund-raising efforts on a matching basis. Minority party candidates who receive at least 5 percent of the popular vote can also get money to reimburse part of their expenses.

To qualify for federal funding, however, candidates must agree to spending ceilings. For the year 2000 presidential primaries the spending limit was about $40 million. Rather than adhere to the ceiling, Republican contender George W. Bush declared in July 1999 that he would not seek federal funding for his primary campaign because he expected to dramatically exceed the federal spending limit. By that time, Bush already had a campaign war chest of $37 million.[96] Other candidates also rejected federal funding, including Republican challenger Steve Forbes, who spent $37 million of his own funds on his 1996 campaign.[97] At a summer 1999 Republican Party straw poll in Iowa, Bush ranked first, and Forbes ranked second among nine contenders for the 2000 Republican nomination.[98]

By September 30, 1999, Bush's campaign receipts swelled to almost $58 million, and Forbes had more than $20 million. By October 21, 1999—months before any primary votes were cast—presidential hopefuls Elizabeth Dole and Dan Quayle dropped out of the race for the Republican nomination. Although each of them had raised about $5 million, it was simply not enough to beat their better-funded opponents.[99] Public funding of presidential campaigns is supposed to provide a level playing field among candidates, but money still holds significant sway in campaign politics. If candidates can refuse public funding in order to exceed the $40,000 ceiling, how effective is the law in creating a level playing field?

## THE COSTS OF CAMPAIGNING

"The candidates want to win," observed Indiana senator Dan Coats. "That means an extraordinary amount of money and an overwhelming presence on television."[100] Often, the candidate who raises and spends the most money becomes the victor on election day.[101]

In 1912 presidential candidates Woodrow Wilson, William Taft, and Theodore Roosevelt spent a total of $3 million on their campaigns. Eighty years later, presidential campaign costs topped $550 million.[102]

Estimates for total spending on all aspects of the 1996 presidential campaign range as high as $800 million.[103]

Candidates for the House of Representatives spent a record-breaking total of $765.3 million during the 1995–96 election cycle. On average, winning House candidates spent more than $681,000 each.[104] Victorious Senate candidates spent more than $3.75 million each, with all Senate candidates spending a total of $287.5 million in 1995–96.[105]

Campaigns at the state and local levels are less expensive. Nonetheless, they can still involve thousands—and even millions—of dollars, especially in large cities.

In the country's early elections, campaigns relied on pamphlets and privately published newspapers to reach the voters. Contemporary candidates communicate through direct mail brochures, ads in magazines and newspapers, television and radio broadcast ads, and Internet sites.

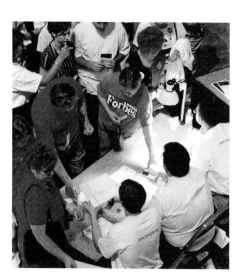

*Iowa Republicans line up to cast their ballots in the Iowa presidential straw poll in Ames, August 14, 1999. More than 20,000 people cast ballots in the nonbinding vote.*

As communications technology expanded, so did political publicity costs. In 1952 Democratic and Republican presidential candidates spent about 30 percent of their campaign budgets on radio and television ads. By 1992 that share ballooned to more than 50 percent.[106] While only about half the candidates for the House of Representatives buy television time, serious Senate candidates spend up to 80 percent of their budgets on broadcast advertising.[107]

Who runs these high-tech campaigns? Candidates for federal and statewide offices frequently hire large cadres of professionals to mold, maintain, and project a public image. "I have been introduced into twenty-first-century campaigning and I don't like it," complained Illinois representative Sidney Yates. "All of a sudden you have to hire a fund-raiser, a media consultant, a press attaché, a mailing specialist."[108]

The list continues to grow. Professional analysts study the electorate, consider campaign developments, and recommend campaign strategies. Public relations firms and advertising agencies present the candidate to the public. They design ads for broadcast and print media, as well as brochures, mailings, billboards, bumper stickers, and buttons. Researchers prepare briefing papers to ensure that candidates can address policy issues with up-to-date facts and figures. Focus groups compare and contrast projected voter response to different presentations of the candidate. Pollsters measure and analyze trends in voter opinion and behavior. Of course, all these services cost money.

With campaign costs spiraling upward, candidates become preoccupied with fund-raising. As West Virginia senator Robert Byrd observed:

> I know something about how senators have to
> go out and spend their time in this grubby, de-
> meaning task of trying to raise money for the re-
> election campaigns. . . . But they have to do it. It
> is a case of survival. Self-survival is one of the
> first laws of nature and they are being forced to
> engage in this unceasing, ever-increasing demand
> for money, money, money—the money chase.[109]

Constant fund-raising exhausts candidates and draws attention away from policies and issues. Moreover, some candidates' staffs, frustrated with legal limits, may seek to evade the law. Either way, there are problems.

## PAC POWER

Despite advances in policing campaign fund-raising, loopholes remain. Besides donating directly to candidates, PACs and other organizations can run their own ads. As long as the expenditures are independent of the candidate's official campaign, the amounts spent are exempt from statutory limits. This means there are no limits.

In the 1996 congressional campaign, for example, New Jersey Republican James Longley benefited from ad spots sponsored by the National Federation of Independent Business, the National Restaurant Association, and a probusiness coalition. Meanwhile, labor groups and organizations for retired people sponsored commercials aiding Longley's challenger, Democrat Thomas Allen. Instead of directly endorsing one candidate or another, the ads heavily criticized each candidate's opponent.[110] With costs for "independent" ad blitzes routinely reaching $500,000 or more, *Time* columnist Jeffrey Birnbaum claims such spending evades federal campaign finance laws.[111]

More seriously, do PACs let special interest groups "buy" influence with elected representatives? The Center for Responsive Politics and Common Cause claim that PAC money results in significant benefits, such as tax benefits for tobacco interests.[112]

Others deny a direct relationship but still acknowledge that PACs have influence. "I take the money from labor, and I have to think twice in voting against their interests," admitted Democratic representative Richard Ottinger of New York. "I shouldn't have to do that."[113]

Yet, as proof that PACs aren't in control, presidential candidate and former Senate majority leader Bob Dole has cited Congress's enactment of wide-reaching social welfare programs. "There aren't any poor PACs or Food Stamp PACs or nutrition PACs or Medicare PACs," he

*Vice President Al Gore stands with AFL-CIO member Victor Perez after Gore won the labor union's endorsement for president in the 2000 election.*

said.[114] In other words, politicians vote for good laws even when they don't stand to gain any campaign contributions.

Not everyone reproaches PACs. "I don't worry about being bought, because I'm not for sale," said Texas senator Phil Gramm. "The truth is I am proud of the PACs and the people who support me."[115]

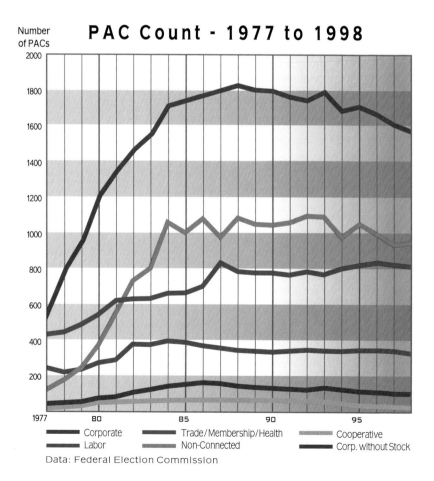

**PAC Count - 1977 to 1998**

Number of PACs

Corporate
Labor
Trade/Membership/Health
Non-Connected
Cooperative
Corp. without Stock

Data: Federal Election Commission

Instead of huge donations from wealthy individuals, PACs collect money from large groups. "PACs facilitate the political participation of hundreds of thousands of individuals who might not otherwise become involved in the election of an individual," claims Virginia senator John Warner.[116] But committees who distribute each PAC's money may have only a few individuals.[117] In other words, even though money is collected from a broad base, the number of people actually making the decisions about which candidate to support is often small. Also, if any corporation or labor union pressures people to "donate," is participation truly voluntary?

In any case, the number of PACs increased dramatically since the 1970s. Almost 4,000 PACs now contribute to presidential and congressional campaigns.[118] Some PACs are linked to corporations, such as the Federal Express Corporation Political Action Committee (FEPAC) and AT&T Corp Political Action Committee (AT&T PAC). Others are tied to labor groups, such as the Ironworkers Political Action League, the Machinists Non-Partisan Political League, the United Auto Workers Voluntary Community Action Program (UAW-V-CAP), and the Service Employees International Union Political Campaign Committee. Trade organization members also sponsor PACs, such as the Association of Trial Lawyers of America Political Action Committee and the American Medical Association Political Action Committee. Still other PACs support specific policy agendas, such as the NRA Political Victory Fund, linked to the National Rifle Association, and the National Right to Life Political Action Committee, which opposes legalized abortion.[119]

In 1996 PACs spent $429.9 million, representing an 11 percent increase over 1994.[120] The top spender was EMILY's List, an organization supporting female Democratic pro-choice candidates.[121] Pro-choice candidates support legalized abortion.

Critics such as political science professor Martin Wattenberg argue that PACs threaten to displace the major parties in functions such as financing and providing organizational services. Rather than appealing to the broad party membership, candidates may focus on narrower issues affecting PACs' special interests.[122]

On the other hand, PAC money may increase access to funding for minority candidates. "If your district is poor, you're not wealthy and you're excluded from affluent circles, it's hard to raise money," observed Democratic representative Eva Clayton of North Carolina.[123]

Norman Ornstein of the American Enterprise Institute for Public Policy Research acknowledges that PACs aren't perfect, but he warns against eliminating or sharply limiting PACs without freeing up other sources of campaign funds. Otherwise, he fears candidates will become even more preoccupied with fund-raising.[124]

### SOFT MONEY

"Soft money" is another gaping legal loophole. Soft money is campaign money that falls outside specific limits in the Federal Election Campaign Act. Instead of directly saying, "Vote for this candidate," soft money spending aims to affect election results in more subtle (and some not so subtle) ways. "Get-out-the-vote" messages may include symbolism or criticism that not only urges voters to get to the polls, but suggests they should vote a certain way. "Party-building" ads may either praise or criticize the Republicans or Democrats without specifically naming a candidate. The implication, however, is that, come election day, the ad sponsors want voters to choose a certain slate of candidates in the voting booth.[125]

Although the amounts of money raised should be reported to the Federal Election Commission, soft money is exempt from federal spending limitations.[126] However, the line between one function and the other often blurs.[127] In 1996 Common Cause complained that both the Democrats and the Republicans improperly promoted presidential candidates with soft money ads. "They used the political parties as conduits [pathways] to run candidate ads," claimed Common Cause president Ann McBride. She called the alleged violations "the most massive violations of the law since Watergate."[128]

"Laundering" of funds—making a donation in someone else's name to evade statutory limitations—is clearly illegal, but it is difficult to police. Additionally, while the law requires disclosure of donations, identifying omissions and prosecuting violators can be difficult.

The federal election laws and numerous state laws seek to ensure a level financial playing field for candidates. Flagrant violations of the law, coupled with questionable use of loopholes, amount to foul play that threatens the integrity of the U.S. election system.

*Republican presidential hopeful Senator John McCain of
Arizona speaks to supporters about campaign finance
reform in Bedford, New Hampshire, in June 1999.*

# SAVING THE GAME

Can campaign politics be changed to avoid foul play? Across the United States, politicians and government scholars are proposing reforms.[129] "The influence of money inordinately affects legislation," says Arizona's Republican senator John McCain. He and Wisconsin's Democratic senator Russ Feingold want to dramatically restrict campaign spending. They prefer an outright ban on contributions to candidates from political action committees. Otherwise, they would like to limit PAC contributions to just $1,000. Agreeing to the limits would mean receiving incentives, such as thirty minutes of free television time and a discount on postage. Not agreeing to the limits would subject candidates to competitive disadvantages.[130]

Although the House of Representatives approved a bill similar to the McCain-Feingold proposal in 1998, the measure was ultimately defeated in the Senate.[131] The Senate blocked a similar bill in October 1999, when backers failed to get the sixty votes needed to stop a filibuster.[132]

"There's no doubt that incumbents don't want to change a system that protects incumbency," McCain observed.[133] Nonetheless, McCain and others have vowed to press forward with efforts to get proposed reforms adopted.[134] Past opponents, such as Republican senator Mitch McConnell from Kentucky, say they are not trying to protect their personal interests. Rather, they see themselves as protecting the First Amendment right to free speech. "When people say we're spending too much, it means they think we're speaking too much," McConnell has said. "I don't think we have too much political debate and discourse."[135]

Freedom of association is another First Amendment right that could conflict with campaign finance reform proposals. "The ability for individuals to get together and decide as a group that they will support certain candidates is a right of free association that's protected by the Constitution," said Laura Murphy of the American Civil Liberties Union.[136]

"In fact," Feingold responded, "the Supreme Court has specifically upheld the kind of voluntary restraints on campaign spending proposed in the McCain-Feingold campaign finance reform legislation and has approved limits upon contributions designed to prevent corruption of our electoral system."[137] In *Buckley v. Valeo,* the U.S. Supreme Court held that certain mandatory provisions of the Federal Election Campaign Act violated the First Amendment, but it upheld other voluntary restrictions.[138]

The Supreme Court has shown it will continue to place limits on the FEC's authority. In 1986 a Colorado Republican Party committee bought radio ads attacking Timothy Wirth, the likely Democratic Party candidate for the Senate. The FEC said the ads violated limits on spending "in connection with the general election campaign of a candidate." Since the Republican nominee had not yet been selected, he or she could not have coordinated the ad spending. But the clear message was to reject the Democratic candidate on election day.

Ten years later, in 1996, the Supreme Court decided against the FEC in *Colorado Republican Federal Campaign Committee v. FEC.*[139] Seven judges found that the FEC could not apply its limit to the party's spending. The ruling confirmed the presence of soft money loopholes in federal law. Thus, it seems that the only way to close the loopholes will be for Congress to pass reform legislation.

In the meantime, various states passed laws to curb campaign spending. In 1996, for example, Arkansas, Missouri, and Idaho passed laws limiting how much donors could give candidates for state office. Alaska also banned corporations, labor unions, and out-of-state political action committees from donating to various state candidates.[140]

In January 2000, the U.S. Supreme Court ruled that Missouri's campaign reform statute was constitutional. In a 6-3 decision, *Nixon v. Shrink Missouri Government PAC* held that the reasoning of *Buckley v. Valeo* applied to state laws limiting campaign contributions. The decision was a positive sign for groups urging campaign finance refrom at both the state and federal levels.[141]

## TOO MUCH REGULATION?

Do more complex requirements merely provide more incentives to circumvent, or get around, the law? "Instead of making unconstitutional and undesirable restrictions on the amount a candidate may raise or spend," California representative John Doolittle mused, "what you need to do is have full and timely disclosure."[142] That means letting the public know right away how much money candidates raise and who the contributors are.

Political science professor Larry Sabato likewise favors less regulation and more disclosure. To reduce political corruption, Sabato argues, "You should encourage direct giving instead of indirect giving, because indirect giving is more difficult to follow."[143] Allowing tax credits or deductions for contributions to political parties could encourage honest reporting.[144] Donors would want to disclose what amount of money they gave in order to get the financial tax benefits. In case of an audit, candidates' records would need to match with the donors' real names, as opposed to "shell" groups. Thus, the public could better track who gives what to whom.

Law school professor Bradley Smith, who has served as a free-market scholar for the Cato Institute, also favors less regulation. Smith says campaign finance reform is basically "an incumbent's protection racket." Challengers who are not already in office must spend huge amounts just to achieve the name recognition already enjoyed by their opponents. Just when a challenger spends enough to become competitive, Smith says, spending limits would "choke off political competition."[145] In other words, challengers could not spend any more money on the campaign, while incumbents would be free to continue spending and surge ahead.

Do you think there should be more or less limitations on campaign fund-raising? Why?

## SHOULD THE PUBLIC PAY?

Federal law already provides supplemental public financing for presidential elections through the voluntary checkoff on income tax returns. For each taxpayer who checks the box, three dollars goes into a fund for presidential elections. Should public financing be expanded to include members of Congress too?

Besides increasing access to political office, public funding proponents claim they would free elected representatives to act in their constituents' interests rather than leaving elected officials financially dependent on special interest groups.[146] Some proposals would provide candidates with free time or dramatically reduced rates for advertising on television and radio stations.[147]

The Maine Clean Election Act provides public financing for legislative and gubernatorial candidates who raise a qualifying amount of seed money. In return, candidates agree not to seek additional private financing.[148] In 1997 Vermont followed Maine's example and enacted its own public financing legislation for gubernatorial elections.[149] Will such laws succeed in their goal of providing clean elections? Time will tell.

## BEEFING UP THE FEC

Critics such as *U.S. News & World Report* columnist Joshua Shenk argue that, like a lap dog, the FEC is reluctant to bite the hand that feeds it.[150] Elected candidates feed the FEC through its annual budget. Past experience shows this is not an unfounded fear.

In 1975 the infant FEC found that North Carolina representative Charlie Rose was innocent of charges of bribery. But congressional representatives were irate that the agency even bothered to investigate the anonymous allegations. The next year, Congress followed through on Representative Wayne Hays's threat to "cut the guts out of your budget," by allotting only 75 percent of the money requested by the FEC.[151]

"Over the years, there's basically been an attempt on the part of people to try to make the FEC ineffective by withholding money," says former Democratic House member Tony Coelho. Even when the FEC follows up on a complaint, the lapse of time and the inability to impose prison sentences can keep candidates from taking campaign finance laws seriously. "There's no fear of the FEC because by the time it gets there, elections are over and there's not much it can do," says Coelho.[152]

Disillusioned by the Justice Department's failure to investigate complaints of wrongdoing against Richard Nixon's reelection campaign, Congress wanted the FEC to be an independent agency not beholden to anyone in the executive branch. But, by holding the purse strings tightly, is Congress now exerting too much control? Since Congress does exercise spending power under the Constitution, is there any practical way to protect the FEC from retaliatory budget cuts? If financial oversight were taken away, to whom would the FEC ultimately be responsible? What, if anything, would you suggest for bolstering the FEC's enforcement powers?

**POLITICS IN PERIL**

Who is hurt by illegal campaign contributions, negative campaigns, and other foul play in election politics? Certainly the challenging candidate has less chance to present his or her views to the public in a fair and impartial way. Ultimately, however, the political process suffers. Instead of "We the People" having a fair and meaningful opportunity to vote for men and women to represent us in government, the real voting choices are narrowed. Drastic violations of campaign finance laws can lead to politicians who are not truly voted into office but rather "bought" there. Elected officials are supposed to work for the public good, not for whoever donated to their campaign—either directly or covertly. If influence is bought and sold, effective cover-ups could prevent the public from learning the truth about whom their elected leaders really answer to.

Even if campaign funds are raised fairly, should elected office be for sale to the highest bidder? In 1996 the candidate spending the most money won 90 percent of the time in races for the House of Representatives and 80 percent of the time in races for the Senate.[153] Strong candidates may well be good at raising money, but the "big bucks" nature of political campaigns can make many voters feel cynical.

With negative campaigning, scare tactics, and scandals, votes may reflect a gut reaction rather than any rational policy preference. In other words, people may vote based on prejudice, fear, or disgust rather than on what they really want in terms of laws and leadership.

The early Federalists feared that leaders would seize power by demagoguery—making false promises that appeal to a crowd's prejudices—or that mobs might seize control and rule thoughtlessly, without regard to legal restraints. The flaws in modern campaign politics probably won't make such extreme fears come to pass. The modern system, however, does not support the founders' ideals of rational decision making and wise policy choices. More than ever, the country needs good leaders who will honestly represent voters' interests, but the process of electing candidates to office does not work well if people lose confidence in the system.

Recent voting statistics suggest these concerns are more than mere speculation. National voter turnout for the 1996 federal elections was only 49 percent—the lowest level since 1920. In contrast, voter turnout for presidential elections in the 1960s was above 60 percent.[154] Also, since 1995 the voter registration process has been made easier than ever. The National Voter Registration Act of 1993 mandates that states requiring preregistration of voters allow mail-in registration. Citizens are also offered an opportunity to register

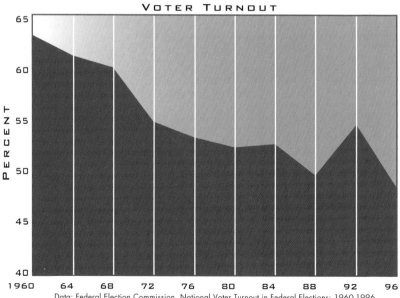

Data: Federal Election Commission, National Voter Turnout in Federal Elections: 1960-1996

when they get a driver's license. From 1994 to 1996, voter registrations increased by 16 million.[155]

Other efforts to increase voter turnout call for mail-in votes rather than in-person voting. When Oregon tried a mail-in vote for a special election in January 1996, voter response soared to 66 percent.[156] If a secure identification system can be established, voting can even take place via the Internet.

Mere inconvenience, however, cannot explain why 50 million registered voters chose not to vote at all in 1996.[157] Admittedly, the higher turnouts of the 1960s coincided with protests over the Vietnam War, racial tensions, and other social unrest. However, important domestic policy issues, such as health care, taxes, public safety, welfare, education, care of the elderly, drugs, and corruption are facing the country. And foreign affairs policy problems can arise at any time. Certainly citizens still have good reason to care deeply about who represents them in government.

One possible reason for low voter turnout is that voters are fed up. Constant news reports about scandals, alleged illegalities, and monetary influences imply that politics—rather than being an esteemed form of public service—is a dishonorable game where everyone cheats at one time or another. One survey reported in *USA Today* revealed that only 43 percent of adults questioned believe honest politicians can get elected.[158] Rather than playing along in a game that appears stacked against the democratic process, disenchanted voters may decide their voice does not count.[159] But "sitting out the game" is not the way to get politicians and their staffs to practice fair play in campaign politics.

## MAKING YOUR VOICE HEARD

What can you do? Even if you are not yet old enough to vote, you can certainly learn about political issues. Write or e-mail elected representatives to tell them what you think needs to be done about different problems. Make your views known through letters to the editor, editorials in teen sections of the newspaper, and other forums.

During political campaigns, learn about the candidates and their positions on the issues. Besides watching television, read newspapers and news magazines. Use the Internet too. Most candidates for federal office—and many state office candidates—have sites on the World Wide Web. Other sites, such as the Federal Election Commission and the Center for Responsive Politics, can provide you with helpful information about federal candidates and their finances.

Pay careful attention to the campaign messages of each party. What points do you think are valid in the political debate? What tactics do you think are foul play? Carefully consider how candidates' willingness to engage in negative campaigning or other practices affects your opinions.

You may find a candidate with whom you agree on every issue. Or you may decide that each candidate has some flaws. In that case, decide which issues concern you the most, and judge which candidates you think would do a better job of representing you and other citizens fairly.

If you are particularly enthusiastic about a candidate, consider becoming involved in his or her campaign. Even though many campaign tasks are now done by professionals, there is still room for volunteers throughout the country. You can learn a lot about the political process by participating at the grassroots level.

Perhaps some day you will choose to run for public office. You may start on the local level by running for city council or the school board. Or you may get involved with one of the major parties and campaign for office at the state or even the national level. Holding public office is by no means easy, but it is a worthwhile opportunity to serve others. If you decide to run, commit to campaigning fairly and lawfully. No matter how worthy your policy aims may be, public service only helps the public if it is truthful and honest.

Finally, when you are old enough, be sure to register and to exercise your right to vote. This book has explored what's fair and what's foul in campaign politics. The system has its flaws, but choosing to sit out the game by not voting won't change anything. Only by taking your role as a voter seriously can you and the democratic system of the United States both come out as winners.

# Resources to Contact

**Government Organizations:**

County and Local Election Officers
Contact your county clerk or
county supervisors to determine
who is responsible for overseeing
county and local elections in your
area.

Federal Election Commission
999 E Street NW
Washington, DC  20463
202-219-4140
800-424-9530
<http://www.fec.gov>

Secretary of State for Your State
The secretary of state generally
oversees state election laws.  His or
her office will be in the capital of
your state.

U.S. Commission on Civil Rights
(works to prevent discrimination
in voting and other illegal
discrimination)
624 Ninth Street NW
Washington, DC  20425
202-376-8312
<http://www.usccr.gov>

**Major Political Parties:**

Democratic National Committee
430 South Capitol Street SE
Washington, DC  20003
202-863-8000
<http://www.democrats.org/index.
html>

Republican National Committee
310 First Street SE
Washington, DC  20003
202-863-8500
<http://www.rnc.org>

**Civic Organizations:**

Center for Responsive Politics
1320 19th Street NW
Washington, DC  20036
202-857-0044
<http://www.opensecrets.org/
home/index.asp>

Common Cause
1250 Connecticut Avenue NW
Suite 600
Washington, DC  20036
800-926-1064
<http://www.commoncause.org>

League of Women Voters of the
United States
1730 M Street NW
Washington, DC  20036
202-429-1965
<http://lwv.org>

Project Vote Smart
One Common Ground
Philipsburg, MT 59858
406-859-8683
888-VOTE SMART
<http://vote-smart.org>

Public Citizen
1600 20th Street NW
Washington, DC  20009
202-5883-1000
<http://www.publiccitizen.org>

# Endnotes

## CHAPTER 1. THE RACE IS ON

[1]CBS News, Election Night Coverage, November 5, 1996.

[2]Ibid.

[3]Victor Kamber, *Poison Politics: Are Negative Campaigns Destroying Democracy?* (New York: Insight Books/Plenum Press, 1997), 273; Kerwin C. Swint, *Political Consultants and Negative Campaigning: The Secrets of the Pros* (Lanham, MD: University Press of America, 1998), 146.

[4]Kamber, 271–275.

[5]Matthew Cooper, "Stewing on the Sidelines," *Newsweek,* Sept. 30, 1996, 30.

## CHAPTER 2. RULES OF THE GAME

[6]Thomas R. Raber, *Presidential Campaign* (Minneapolis: Lerner Publications Company, 1988), 7, quoting Franklin Roosevelt.

[7]U.S. Constitution (Const.), art. 2, sec. 1; amend. 22.

[8]U.S. Const., art. 1; sec. 2–3.

[9]U.S. Code vol. 2, sec. 431 et seq.

## CHAPTER 3. CHOOSING SIDES

[10]Keith Polakoff, *Political Parties in American History* (New York: John Wiley & Sons, 1981), 23.

[11]Edmund Lindop, *Political Parties* (New York: Twenty-First Century Books, 1996), 7.

[12]Ibid., 280–84.

[13]Frank Smallwood, *The Other Candidates: Third Parties in Presidential Elections* (Hanover, NH: University Press of New England, 1983), 14–15; Polakoff, 120–22.

[14]Lindop, 45.

[15]John F. Bibby and L. Sandy Maisel, *Two Parties—Or More? The American Party System* (Boulder, CO: Westview Press, 1998), 26–27.

[16]Ibid., 33–34, 40–42.

[17]Lindop, 46–47.

[18]Smallwood, 234.

[19]William Keefe, *Parties, Politics, and Public Policy in America* (7th ed.; Washington, DC: CQ Press, 1994), 290–93.

[20]Ibid., 303–08.

[21]Stephen Ansolabehere and Shanto Iyengar, *Going Negative: How Political Advertisements Shrink & Polarize the Electorate* (New York: Free Press, 1995), 10.

[22]Keefe, 228–29.

## CHAPTER 4. SCORING POINTS

[23]Gil Troy, *See How They Ran: The Changing Role of the Presidential Candidate* (Rev. ed.; Cambridge, MA: Harvard University Press, 1996), 7.

[24]Ibid., 63–65.

[25]Ibid., 210–11.

[26]Ibid., 265.

[27]Janet Majure, *Elections* (San Diego, CA: Lucent Books, Inc., 1996), 61.

[28]Paul Herrnson, *Congressional Elections: Campaigning at Home and in Washington* (Washington, DC: CQ Press, 1995), 160.

[29]Federal Election Commission, *Twenty Year Report,* (Washington, DC, GPO, April 1995), 29.

[30]Robert A. Devine, et al., *America: The People and the Dream,* vol. I (Glenview, IL: Scott, Foresman and Co., 1991), 509, quoting Franklin Roosevelt.

[31]Kamber, 58.

[32]Darrell West, *Air Wars: Television Advertising in Election Campaigns, 1952–1992* (Washington, DC: Congressional Quarterly, 1993), 43.

[33]Steven Colford, "What's Ahead; Read My Lips: Taxes," *Advertising Age,* Nov. 7, 1988, 1; Alexander Cockburn, "Cap'n Bushy on the Burning Deck," *The Nation,* November 9, 1992, 531.

[34]Troy, 225–26.

[35]Bruce Tomaso, "Gore Says Budget Surplus Should Go for Social Security, Medicare," Knight-Ridder/Tribune Business News Service, July 29, 1999; *see also,* Alan S. Blinder, "Save It," *The New Republic,* August 9, 1999, 25.

[36] "The Budget Surplus: Don't Blow It," *Business Week,* July 12, 1999, 25.

[37]Barry Bluestone, "Spend It: What to Do with a $2.9 Trillion Surplus?" *The New Republic,* August 9, 1999, 23.

[38]William F. Buckley, Jr., "Women Versus Men?" *National Review,* December 9, 1996, 75.

[39]Will Manley, "Soccer Mom Nation," *Booklist,* January 1, 1997, 782; Margaret Carlson, "The Rules from 1996," *Time,* November 11, 1996, 42.

## CHAPTER 5. CALLING THE SHOTS

[40]Gloria Borger, "Private Lives, Public Figures," *U.S. News & World Report,* May 18, 1987, 20.

[41]Walter Shapiro, "Fall from Grace: Seven Days in May End with a Front Runner's Implosion," *Time,* May 18, 1987, 16, quoting Gary Hart.

[42]Borger, 20, discussing Senator Wilbur Mills, Representative Wayne Hays, Representative Robert Bauman, and Senator Thomas Dodd.

[43]Ibid., quoting historian Doris Kearns Goodwin ("The insulation that develops among candidates and presidents makes them think they're beyond ordinary rules.") and historian Carl Brauer ("It's not what the candidate does, but whether he tries to hide it.").

[44]Ibid.

[45]*New York Times v. Sullivan,* 376 U.S. 254 (1964).

[46] "Where Clinton Leads by a Mile—and Where It's Close," *Time,* April 15, 1996, 27.

[47]Nancy Gibbs and Michael Duffy, *Time,* September 16, 1996, 40.

[48]Deborah Kalb, "Dole Must Close 'Gender Gap' to Avoid Clinton Landslide," *Congressional Quarterly Weekly Report,* October 26, 1996, 3085.

[49] "How Gallup Poll Did in Predicting Previous Elections," Knight-Ridder/Tribune News Service, September 11, 1996.

[50]Everett Carll Ladd, "The Election Polls," *Current,* February 1997, 26; "Whoops!" *Time for Kids,* Fall 1996 (special issue), 5.

[51]Ibid., Susan Crabtree, "Why Most Media Polls Were Grossly Inaccurate," *Insight on the News,* December 2, 1996, 16.

[52]Robert Erikson, Robert and Lee Sigelman, "Poll-based Forecasts of Midterm Congressional Election Outcomes: Do the Pollsters Get It Right?" *Public Opinion Quarterly,* winter 1995, 589.

[53]Ibid.

[54]Ibid., "Vanishing Voters," *Time for Kids,* November 15, 1996, 3.

[55]Crabtree, 16–17, quoting Dan Hazelwood.

[56]Ibid., quoting Mark Mellman.

[57]Martha Moore, "Critics Believe TV Devalues Western Votes," *USA Today,* November 5, 1996.

[58]Ibid.

[59]Shankar Vedantam, "Polls May Be More Accurate Than Elections, Wider Participation," Knight-Ridder/Tribune News Service, September 11, 1996.

## CHAPTER 6. HITTING BELOW THE BELT

[60]West, 66–67.

[61]Ibid.

[62]Karen S. Johnson-Cartee and Gary A. Copeland, *Negative Political Advertising: Coming of Age* (Hillsdale, NJ: Lawrence Erlbaum Associates, Publishing, 1991), 133–34.

[63]Ansolabehere and Iyengar, 4.

[64]West, 114.

[65]Troy, 13.

[66]Johnson-Cartee and Copeland, 6.

[67]Troy, 15.

[68]Adam Clymer, "Labor-Backed Challenger Has Incumbent in Trouble," *New York Times,* October 11, 1996; Laura Meissner, "Hoke-Kucinich Debate Leaves Listener Pondering," *Cleveland Plain Dealer,* October 28, 1996; "Election '96: As Hoke Airs Critical Ad, Mayor White, Council Plan to Honor Kucinich by Renaming a Building after Him," *Cleveland Plain Dealer,* October 18, 1996.

[69]Tamala M. Edwards, "Oops! The Top Gaffes of Election '98," *Time,* November 16, 1998, 33; "Welcome to the Mudbath," *Economist,* October 31, 1998, 27.

[70]Alan Greenblatt, "Negative Campaigning: Denounced, Denied, and Indispensable?" *Congressional Quarterly Weekly Report,* October 31, 1998, 2950.

[71]Ansolabehere and Iyengar, 72–82, 96–98.

[72]Johnson-Cartee and Copeland, 15.

[73]Ibid.

[74]Michael Pfau and Henry C. Kenski, *Attack Politics: Strategy and Defense* (New York: Praeger, 1990), 1.

[75]Ibid., 13.

[76]Troy, 154–55, 208–09.

[77]Bill Hewitt, et al., "Clinton on Trial," *People Weekly,* February 10, 1992, 32; *see also* Steven Roberts, "Defusing the Bombshell," *U.S. News & World Report,* February 3, 1992, 30.

**CHAPTER 7. PAY TO PLAY?**

[78]Kevin Fedarko, "The Foreign Foul-Up," *Time,* October 28, 1996, 42; Howard Fineman and Mark Hosenball, "The Asian Connection," *Newsweek,* October 28, 1996, 24, 27; Marcy Gordon, "Gore's Ties to Buddhist Sect Get Closer Look," *USA Today,* December 24, 1996.

[79]Marcy Gordon, "Clinton: Donor's Letter Just Suggested Policy," *USA Today,* December 3, 1996; Michael Isikoff and Mark Hosenball, "'A Bottomless Pit,'" *Newsweek,* November 18, 1996, 24; Fedarko, 43.

[80]Susan Page, "Scandal Dogs Clinton Briefing," *USA Today,* January 29, 1997, 7A.

[81]David Espo, "Gingrich Assures, Reassures Colleagues," *USA Today,* January 7, 1997; Jill Lawrence, "Gingrich Probe, Reno Pose PR Conundrums," *USA Today,* December 4, 1996; "Letter about Gingrich Is Questioned," *USA Today,* January 2, 1997; "Gingrich Payment," *USA Today,* January 29, 1997.

[82]*Buckley v. Valeo,* 424 U.S. 1 (1976).

[83]Federal Election Commission, *Twenty Year Report,* 2.

[84]Ibid., 6–8.

[85]Robin Kolodny, *Pursuing Majorities: Congressional Campaign Committees in American Politics* (Norman, OK: University of Oklahoma Press, 1998), 125.

[86]Robert J. Wagner and Angela E. Lauria, eds., *The World Almanac of U.S. Politics,* 1997–1999 ed. (Mahwah, NJ: World Almanac Books, 1997), 23.

[87]Public Law 92–225, section 104, 92nd Cong., 2nd sess. (1972).

[88]Ibid., sec. 608.

[89]Ibid., sec. 301–311.

[90]Federal Election Commission, *Twenty Year Report,* 2–4.

[91]*See generally* Carl Bernstein and Bob Woodward, *All the President's Men* (New York: Simon & Schuster, 1974); Suzanne Coil, *Campaign Financing: Politics and the Power of Money* (Brookfield, CT: Millbrook Press, 1994), 12–15.

[92]Public Law 93-443.

[93]Public Law 94-283, adopted in response to *Buckley v. Valeo,* 424 U.S. 1 (1976).

[94]The Federal Election Campaign Act is codified at 2 U.S. Code, sec. 431 et seq.

[95]2 U.S. Code, sec. 431 et seq. *See generally* Federal Election Commission, *Campaign Guide for Congressional Candidates and Committees* (Washington, DC, GPO, 1995).

[96]Don Van Natta Jr., "Bush Forgoes Federal Funds and Has No Spending Limit," *New York Times,* July 16, 1999.

[97]Ibid.

[98]Richard L. Berke, "Bush Triumphs in Iowa Straw Poll," *New York Times,* August 15, 1999.

[99]Federal Election Commission, *Financial Activity of 1999–2000 Presidential Campaigns through September 30, 1999,* <http://www.fed.gov/finance/prsq399.htm>; *See also* Katherine Q. Seelye, "Low on Cash, Dole Withdraws from GOP Race," *New York Times,* October 21, 1999.

[100]Walter Shapiro, "Few Rush to Reform Campaign Finances," *USA Today,* December 18, 1996.

[101]Thomas Ferguson, "Political Contributions Determine Election Outcomes," in *Voting Behavior,* edited by Paul Winters, (San Diego, CA: Greenhaven Press, Inc., 1996), 64.

[102]Lindop, 48.

[103]"Democracy vs. Free Speech?" *The Progressive,* January 1997, 8.

[104]Federal Election Commission, *Congressional Fund-raising and Spending Up Again in 1996,* Press Release, April 14, 1997. For the 1998 elections, congressional campaign spending declined, but it still exceeded $700 million. Combined spending by rivals Al D'Amato and Charles Schumer in the New York Senate race discussed in Chapter 6 topped $40 million. Federal Election Commission, "1998 Congressional Financial Activity Declines," Press Release, December 29, 1998.

[105]Ibid.

[106]West, 7–8.

[107]Keefe, 153.

[108]Ibid., 170.

[109]Coil, 16–17.

[110]Jeffrey H. Birnbaum, "Beating the System," *Time,* October 21, 1996, 32.

[111]Ibid.

[112]Mark J. Rozell and Clyde Wilcox, *Interest Groups in American Campaigns: The New Face of Electioneering* (Washington, DC: Congressional Quarterly, Inc., 1999), 153.

[113]Keefe, 164.

[114]Coil, 75.

[115]Keefe, 164.

[116]Ibid., 164.

[117]Coil, 58.

[118]Federal Election Commission, *FEC Releases Semi-Annual Federal PAC Count,* July 25, 1997, <http://www.fec.gov.press/semipac.html> (3875 as of July 1, 1997).

[119]All these PACs ranked among the top 50 spenders for the period 1997–1998. Federal Election Committee, "Top 50 PACs: Disbursements 1997–98," <http://www.fec.gov/press/pacdis98.htm>.

[120] "Big-spending PACs," *USA Today,* June 3, 1997, 1A.

[121]Ibid. EMILY's List spent $12.5 million for the 1996 elections. EMILY's List also ranked first in spending for the 1998 elections. FEC, "Top 50 PACS."

[122]Martin Wattenberg, *The Decline of American Political Parties, 1952–1992* (Rev. ed.; Cambridge, MA: Harvard University Press, 1994), 109–10.

[123]Beth Donovan, "Black Caucus: PAC Funds a Must for Minorities," Washington, DC: *Congressional Quarterly,* September 25, 1993, 2523.

[124]Eric Uslaner, ed., *American Political Parties: A Reader* (Itasca, IL: F. E. Peacock Publishing, Inc., 1993), 525–27.

[125]Anthony Corrado, *Paying for Presidents: Public Financing in National Elections* (New York: Twentieth Century Fund Press, 1993), 96–100.

[126]Federal Election Commission, *Financial Disclosure Reports of Major Political Parties Show Increases in 'Soft Money' Contributions,* September 22, 1997, <http://www.fec.gov/press/pty698.html>, notes that during the first six months of 1997, an "off" year for federal elections, Republicans raised $21.7 million and Democrats took in $13.7 million in soft money.

[127]Joe Frolik, "The Money Trail," *Plain Dealer Sunday Magazine,* January 25, 1998, 8.

[128]Jill Lawrence, "Money Burns a Hole in Politics," *USA Today,* December 10, 1996.

## CHAPTER 8. SAVING THE GAME

[129]John Berlau, "Spending Limits a Good Idea Whose Time May Not Come," *Insight on the News,* March 10, 1997, 16.

[130]Senate Bill (S); see also Brookings Working Group on Campaign Finance Reform, <http://www.brook.edu/gs/campaign/bills.html>.

[131]John McCain, "The Scandal in Our Midst," *Newsweek,* August 17, 1998, 13; Alison Mitchell, "McCain Renews Push for Debate on Campaign Finance Overhaul," *New York Times,* July 19, 1999.

[132]Alison Mitchell, "Vote on Campaign Finances Is Blocked by Senate GOP," *New York Times,* October 20, 1999.

[133]Berlau, 16–17.

[134]Mitchell.

[135]Ibid.

[136]Ibid.

[137]Russ Feingold, "Few Are Against Campaign Reform," *USA Today,* December 13, 1996.

[138]*Buckley v. Valeo,* 424 U.S. 1 (1976).

[139]*Colorado Republican Federal Campaign Committee v. FEC,* 518 U.S. 604 (June 26, 1996).

[140] "What States Are Doing to Reform Campaign-Finance Laws," Knight-Ridder/Tribune News Service, December 9, 1997.

[141]*Nixon v. Shrink Missouri Government PAC,* No. 98-963,—U.S.—(Jan. 24, 2000); *see also* CNN.com, "Court Affirms States' Power to Impose Campaign Contribution Limits," <CNN.com/2000/us/01/24/scotus.contributions.ap>.

[142]Berlau, 16–17.

[143]Ibid., 16–17.

[144]Coil, 92–93.

[145]Bradley Smith, "Why Campaign Finance Reform Never Works," *Wall Street Journal,* March 19, 1997.

[146] "Democracy v. Free Speech?" 8–9; Coil, 86–88.

[147]Herrnson, 249–51.

[148]*Maine Revised Statutes, Annotated,* Title 21A, sec. 1121 et seq. (West 2000).

[149] "What States Are Doing To Reform Campaign-Finance Laws," Knight-Ridder/Tribune News Service, December 9, 1997.

[150]Joshua Wolf Shenk, "Designed for Impotence," *U.S. News & World Report,* January 20, 1997, 30.

[151]Ibid., 30.

[152]Ibid., 32.

[153]Stanley C. Brubaker, "The Limits of Campaign Spending Limits," *The Public Interest,* Fall 1998, 33.

[154]Federal Election Commission, "National Voter Turnout in Federal Elections: 1960-1996," <http://www.fec.gov/pages/htmlto5.html>.

[155]Ibid., "Vanishing Voters," *Time for Kids.*

[156]Phil Keisling, "What If We Held an Election and Nobody Came?" *Washington Monthly,* March 1996, 40.

[157]FEC, "National Voter Turnout."

[158] "A Nation of Cynics?" *USA Today,* January 28, 1998.

[159]Ansolabehere and Iyengar, 112–13.

*The MTV Rock the Vote bus sits in front of the Rock 'n Roll Hall of Fame and Museum in Cleveland, Ohio.*

# Glossary

**ballot:** the formal slate of candidates in an election

**candidate:** person who runs for public office

**election:** legally organized procedure for voters to choose between competing candidates for public office

**electoral college:** group of electors committed to casting their votes for president and vice president of the United States, depending on who wins a majority of the popular vote in their respective states

**filibuster:** continuous speech under the Senate's rules for unlimited debate to prevent a measure from coming up for a vote

**grass roots:** the basic level of society or an organization

**ideology:** framework for political ideas

**incumbent:** a person already holding political office

**independent:** not committed to a political party

**inflation:** a continuing rise in the general price level of goods and services

**landslide:** election victory where the candidate wins by a large margin over the opponent

**malicious intent:** intent to commit an unlawful act or cause harm without legal justification or excuse; the desire to cause pain, injury, or distress to another person

**media:** avenues by which people receive news, such as newspapers, magazines, radio, television, and the Internet

**mudslinging:** negative campaigning that tarnishes another candidate's personal image, usually by hurling personal accusations against him or her

**negative campaigning:** campaign strategies that emphasize the negative aspects of the opponent so that people will vote against him or her come election day

**nominate:** to propose a candidate for election to office

**nonpartisan:** not affiliated with or supported by a political party. Many judicial elections and some mayoral races are nonpartisan, for example.

**platform:** formal statement of policies that a candidate or a political party supports

**political party:** organization whose primary goal is to get its candidates elected to public office

**poll:** depending on the context in which the term is used, either a public opinion survey or the place where people go to vote

**prosecute:** to bring legal action against someone for redress or punishment of a crime or violation of the law

**soft money:** money outside the limits of the Federal Election Campaign Act, such as funds spent for "party-building" efforts

**sound bite:** brief statement—usually 12 seconds or less—that summarizes a candidate's position on an issue

**status quo:** the existing situation

**straw poll:** an unofficial count to indicate the relative strength of opposing candidates or issues

**tariff:** a tax charged on goods that are imported or exported

**third party:** a political party other than one of the two major parties

**voter registration:** the process by which a person's name is added to the list of qualified voters. On election day, officials check each person's name against the list before they let the person vote.

**war chest:** a fund that is earmarked for a specific campaign

# Selected Bibliography

Ansolabehere, Stephen, and Shanto Iyengar. *Going Negative: How Political Advertisements Shrink & Polarize the Electorate.* New York: Free Press, 1995.

Bibby, John F., and L. Sandy Maisel. *Two Parties—Or More? The American Party System.* Boulder, CO: Westview Press, 1998.

Chorlian, Meg, ed. "Elections in America." *Cobblestone: The History Magazine for Young People,* vol. 17, no. 7 (October 1996).

Coil, Suzanne M. *Campaign Financing: Politics and the Power of Money.* Brookfield, CT: Millbrook Press, 1994.

Drew, Elizabeth. *Corruption in American Politics: What Went Wrong and Why.* New York: Birch Lane Press, 1999.

Herrnson, Paul S. *Congressional Elections: Campaigning at Home and in Washington.* Washington, DC: CQ Press, 1995.

Kamber, Victor. *Poison Politics: Are Negative Campaigns Destroying Democracy?* New York: Insight Books/Plenum Press, 1997.

Keefe, William. *Parties, Politics, and Public Policy in America.* 7th ed. Washington, DC: CQ Press, 1994.

Kolodny, Robin. *Pursuing Majorities: Congressional Campaign Committees in American Politics.* Norman, OK: University of Oklahoma Press, 1998.

Kronenwetter, Michael. *Political Parties of the United States.* Springfield, NJ: Enslow Publications, 1996.

Lindop, Edmund. *Political Parties.* New York: Twenty-First Century Books, 1996.

Majure, Janet. *Elections.* San Diego, CA: Lucent Books, Inc., 1996.

Raber, Thomas R. *Presidential Campaign.* Minneapolis: Lerner Publications Company, 1988.

Rozell, Mark J., and Clyde Wilcox. *Interest Groups in American Campaigns: The New Face of Electioneering.* Washington, DC: Congressional Quarterly Inc., 1999.

Swint, Kerwin C. *Political Consultants and Negative Campaigning: The Secrets of the Pros.* Lanham, MD: University Press of America, 1998.

Troy, Gil. *See How They Ran: The Changing Role of the Presidential Candidate.* Rev. ed. Cambridge, MA: Harvard University Press, 1996.

Wattenberg, Martin P. *The Decline of American Political Parties,* 1952–1996. Cambridge, MA: Harvard University Press, 1998.

West, Darrell M. *Air Wars: Television Advertising in Election Campaigns, 1952–1992.* Washington, DC: Congressional Quarterly, Inc., 1993.

Winters, Paul A. *Voting Behavior.* San Diego, CA: Greenhaven Press, Inc., 1996.

# Index

## About the Author

**Kathiann M. Kowalski** is the author of dozens of stories and articles for young people and of *Hazardous Waste Sites,* a Lerner Pro/Con book that won the Society of School Librarians International award. She received her bachelor's degree in political science from Hofstra University and her law degree from Harvard Law School, where she was an editor of the *Harvard Law Review.* In addition to writing, she has fifteen years of experience practicing law.

## Photo Acknowledgements

The photographs in this book are reproduced through the courtesy of: AP/World Wide Photos, pp. 6, 14, 39,75,81, 86; Reuters/Brian Snyder/ Archive Photos, p. 9; © Arnold Sachs/CNP/Archive Photos, p. 10; © Joseph Sohm/Corbis, pp.13, 18; © Jim Levitt/Impact Visuals, p. 19; Reuters Newmedia Inc./Corbis, p. 21; Museum of the City of New York/Archive Photos, p. 22; © Bettmann/Corbis, pp. 24 (left), 36, 38, 56, 60, 70; National Gallery of Art, Washington, D.C., p. 24 (right); Archive Photos, pp. 25, 28, 46, 53; © Corbis, pp. 27, 29; © AFP/Corbis, pp. 33, 50; U.S. Office of War Information, courtesy of Franklin D. Roosevelt Library, p. 42; © Jim West, pp. 48, 72; © Jack Ainsworth/Impact Visuals, p. 49; © Rick Reinhard/ Impact Visuals, p. 67; Reuters/Archive Photos, p. 78; © Piet van Lier/Impact Visuals, p. 105.

Front cover, © IPS; back cover, © Joseph Sohm/ChromoSohm Inc./Corbis